IMAGES
of America

SCOTTY'S CASTLE

The Union Pacific Railroad issued this map in 1928 in an advertising brochure for Death Valley winter tours by rail and motor shortly after the Furnace Creek Inn was opened for tourist business. Note the location of "Scotty's Ranch" at the top of the map. After Scotty's Castle was opened to the public, some of these tours would include excursions to the castle as well. (Author's collection.)

ON THE COVER: Scotty's Castle is one of the major attractions visited in Death Valley National Park. Here, the main house is to the left of the arched wooden gate separating the two main buildings. The annex with its large distinctive turret is to the right. The extensive tile work and handmade wrought iron features are evident throughout the castle. (Murray.)

IMAGES
of America

SCOTTY'S CASTLE

Robert P. Palazzo

ARCADIA
PUBLISHING

Published by Arcadia Publishing
Charleston, South Carolina

Library of Congress Control Number: 2015959872

For all general information, please contact Arcadia Publishing:
Telephone 843-853-2070
Fax 843-853-0044
E-mail sales@arcadiapublishing.com
For customer service and orders:
Toll-Free 1-888-313-2665

Visit us on the Internet at www.arcadiapublishing.com

This book is dedicated to Joseph Paolo Palazzo, whose lifelong passion for Scotty's Castle is unsurpassed and who provided constant inspiration for this work, and to my wife, Vivianne, who has cheerfully endured Death Valley the place and all my Death Valley books.

CONTENTS

ACKNOWLEDGMENTS

I would like to thank the following individuals who provided either encouragement, support, and/or help during the course of this project: Dale Alberstone, Thomas A. Baier, the curators and staff of Death Valley National Park Museum, Michael Dawson, John DeSimio, Dr. Katherine Duggan, Dr. Suzanne Frederick, Tom Gibilisco, Rick Gibson, Dana Gioia, Henry Golas, Michael Hecht, the late Reginald Hill, Eric James, Gregory Krisilas, Denny Kruska, Jim Lorenzo, Donald J. Palazzo, Ellen Palazzo, Stephen Palazzo, James E. Smith, Laura Stalker, and the staff of the Huntington Library, Robert Varlotta, and Matt and Allyson Wale. I also want to thank "T" and "J," who wish to remain anonymous, but they know who they are. In addition, my editor Ryan Easterling has provided valuable comments and help. Of course, I am indebted to my wife, Vivianne, who once again had to endure the long and time-consuming process of book authorship, who did so with a smile and continued to offer valuable suggestions and insights.

The following abbreviations are used for photographs: NPS for National Park Service, Death Valley National Park and Murray for those taken by and courtesy of the late Tom Murray.

All photographs are courtesy of the author's collection unless noted otherwise.

INTRODUCTION

One of the most visited and well-known sights in Death Valley National Park is Scotty's Castle. The history of Scotty's Castle and its namesake, Walter E. Scott, known as "Death Valley Scotty," is an improbable story. As with most things about Scotty, nothing is as it seems. Scotty's Castle is not a castle—rather a Spanish hacienda. It did not belong to Scotty; it was owned and built by Albert M. Johnson and his wife, Bessie. In fact, Scotty's Castle is not even its name. The correct name is Death Valley Ranch.

The building itself is a Spanish-style mansion or hacienda that would not have garnered undue attention if it were located in any upscale area of the United States. Its remote location in Death Valley and its association with the infamous Death Valley Scotty assured its place in the public's consciousness.

Visitors to Death Valley and Scotty's Castle often ask, "Who is Death Valley Scotty?" There are many possible replies. The answer often depends on who is responding to the question. At various times, Scotty been referred to as a prospector, cowboy, entertainer, member of *Buffalo Bill's Wild West Show*, actor, con man, publicity seeker, criminal, scam artist, bunco man, wealthy miner, philanthropist, advisor to motion picture studios, consummate host, lively companion, good friend, and the list goes on. In truth, no one description is accurate—he was a bit of each.

Death Valley Scotty was born Walter Edward Perry Scott in Cynthiana, Kentucky, in 1872. He joined *Buffalo Bill's Wild West Show* as a cowboy and toured with them for 12 years. After leaving the show in 1902, Scotty was grubstaked by New York banker Julian M. Gerard, whom he conned for years with stories of a valuable mining discovery. When Gerard became disillusioned, Scotty turned to Albert M. Johnson, with whom he formed a lifelong friendship and ultimately was the real source of Scotty's wealth.

Scotty became nationally known in 1905 when he chartered a train (with Johnson's money) to break the Los Angeles-to-Chicago speed record. His attempt was successful, and the resulting publicity put him in the national spotlight, in which he stayed for the remainder of his life.

Death Valley Scotty was a true marketing genius. His biggest (and only) client was himself. He would put a positive spin on anything and was a firm believer of the adage "there is no such thing as bad publicity." Scotty learned a lot from his time with Buffalo Bill. When Scotty was a cowboy in *Buffalo Bill's Wild West Show*, Buffalo Bill was as at the pinnacle of his popularity and success. Bill was known around the world and was the world's first international superstar entertainer.

Scotty was famous for being famous long before it was popularized by today's reality stars. He promoted himself as a "Man of Mystery" with a secret gold mine that provided him with a source of untold wealth. When investors and nosy members of the public tried to pin Scotty down, its location would change and shift with the wind. No one was ever able to see it or find it (as it did not exist).

When investors became too curious about the mine, Scotty staged a fake robbery known as the "Battle of Wingate Pass" to scare them from pursuing the matter. The robbery backfired when Scotty's brother was shot and wounded. There were resulting lawsuits in which Scotty was forced to confess he was a liar and a crook. Despite these confessions, the aura and mystery surrounding Scotty did not abate, and while the public soon forgot the confessions, it did not forget Scotty and his mine.

Albert Johnson was upset with this turn of events. However, he noticed that when he was in Death Valley checking on his "investments" with Scotty, his health improved. Johnson was in a devastating train accident when he was younger and suffered a great deal. The climate of Death Valley eased his physical pain, and the camaraderie of Scotty relaxed his mind from his business enterprises. Johnson enjoyed his visits to Death Valley so much, he wanted a place to stay, so he bought the Steininger Ranch in Grapevine Canyon.

In 1922, construction began on three buildings. The largest building was a two-story, 32-by-96-foot stucco house. The house had a kitchen, storage rooms, a room downstairs for Scotty, and two large apartments upstairs for the Johnsons and their guests. Another stucco building consisted of a workshop and garage. The third building on the side of a hill was the cookhouse. These buildings were functional, basic, and unimpressive; however, they did contain very modern features such as a generator, refrigeration plant, and indoor plumbing that were suitable for wealthy people of the day.

It was later decided to remodel the stucco buildings, which ultimately became the "castle." Extensive work to both the exterior and interior included gutting the interior of the existing main stucco building, excavating a basement, constructing several hundred feet of tunnels to outbuildings, and providing access to the water, sewer, and electric lines. New walls were built, and the spaces between them were filled with powder that expanded and dried when water was added, resulting in excellent insulation for both summer and winter.

In 1929, Johnson built Scotty a rustic five-room redwood house at Lower Vine Ranch, which, although lacking conveniences, Scotty found preferable to the constant activity at the castle.

Construction on the castle stopped in 1931 due to the financial setbacks Johnson suffered during the stock market crash in 1929 and problems with the title. Before Death Valley became a national monument in 1933, a preliminary survey disclosed that the castle was not located on land that Johnson owned. Johnson tried incessantly to purchase the land on which the castle was built from the United States. After several failed bills in Congress, Johnson finally was allowed to trade some of his acreage to the government and purchase the castle land, which included the Upper and Lower Vine Ranches. Since the Congressional bill provided "to grant a patent to Albert M. Johnson and Walter Scott," Johnson made Scotty sign a document relinquishing all rights to the property.

When Death Valley became a national monument in 1933, the roads were improved, and transportation to Death Valley became easier. More tourists visited Death Valley to meet Death Valley Scotty and see his castle. Accommodations were made at the castle for these tourists, and Scotty took great pleasure in entertaining his "guests." Bessie Johnson first organized informal tours of the castle and later more structured tours, for which tourists paid $1 and had a guide.

Bessie Johnson died in 1943, and when Albert died in 1948, his will provided that ownership of the castle be transferred to the Gospel Foundation of California with the proviso that Scotty would be allowed to live in the castle for the remainder of his life. Scotty died in 1954 and was buried on a hill overlooking the castle. The National Park Service purchased the castle and surrounding property for $850,000 from the Gospel Foundation of California in 1970. The castle is now a part of Death Valley National Park (created in 1994) and visited by upwards of 100,000 people a year.

One

CASTLE CONSTRUCTION

The Scotty's Castle that is known today was built on the old Steininger Ranch in Upper Grapevine Canyon that Albert and Bessie Johnson bought from Jacob Steininger in 1917. The buildings at the Steininger Ranch consisted of a wooden cabin and three wooden-sided canvas tents. After spending a few winters in the rustic cabin, Bessie Johnson felt she deserved better accommodations if she was expected to accompany Albert to Death Valley on future trips. Accordingly, construction started on three stucco buildings in 1922. The largest was a two-story, 3,000-square-foot house with a kitchen, storage rooms, a room for Scotty, and a large apartment for the Johnsons and another for guests. One of the smaller buildings was used for a garage and workshop, and the other served as a cookhouse.

A few years later, Johnson undertook renovation of the three stucco buildings, charitably considered to be "architecturally inartistic." Johnson engaged Frank Lloyd Wright to come up with some designs, which were determined to be too expensive, although Wright's idea for a front swimming pool and the circular pool and fountain were ultimately incorporated into the final design. In 1925, Johnson hired a classmate of Bessie's from Stanford, Matt Roy Thompson, to be the general superintendent and proposed arches and tile work similar to that found at the Stanford University campus. In 1926, designer Charles Alexander MacNeilledge was hired to direct overall planning, and Martin D. de Dubovay was recruited to provide technical assistance in the wood carvings, iron fixtures, and tiles.

From 1925 to 1931, the existing stucco structures were gutted and rebuilt, and the grounds were expanded to include the two-story house connected with a two-story annex, a two apartment guesthouse, stables, cookhouse, large garage, supply room, and office. The large garage contained workshops, bunkhouse, chicken coop, and assay office. The complex also had a service station, gatehouse, chimes tower, powerhouse, solar hot water heater, and swimming pool.

In 1931, during the Great Depression, Johnson's business reversed, and problems with the title to the castle stopped work. Though it may not seem so, construction of Scotty's Castle was never completed.

At the time of this photograph, the small wooden shack located in Grapevine Canyon still bears a sign indicating it was the "Original Castle." It formed a part of the original Steininger Ranch that Albert Johnson bought in 1917. Before the castle was constructed, the ranch buildings served as the Johnsons' headquarters and later the living quarters for Scotty.

Scotty is in front of the original cabin, which is located next to the current castle. Written on the back is the following: "We figgered out every detail of that there Castle right here in this 10 by 14 foot shack." The "we" includes his late partner, Chicago millionaire Albert M. Johnson. They assembled European artisans, American laborers, and Indians and hauled the materials and furnishings through the barren lands that surround Death Valley. (Murray.)

This is a representation of the original design of the castle, which was rendered by the designer Charles Alexander MacNeilledge of Los Angeles. Death Valley Scotty, with tongue in cheek, would tell the tourists that the castle would be surrounded by a moat with man-eating sharks and a drawbridge.

The first phase of the construction of the castle involved the remodeling of the two-story stucco box-like building that was being used as a storage room and occasionally as a "hideaway camp" by both Albert Johnson and Scotty. This photograph of Death Valley Scotty standing next to Mrs. Dane Coolidge shows the progress of the first remodel around the end of 1926.

The renovation and remodeling of the original stucco buildings was well under way when this photograph was taken during May 1927. Here, the main house is covered in scaffolding, and the wood framing is being covered. It was about this time that Albert Johnson met Martin D. de Dubovay in a Los Angeles rug shop. Dubovay was hired to provide architectural and artistic assistance to MacNeilledge.

Death Valley Scotty sits on a wooden crate and aimlessly whittles on a piece of wood he picked up at the castle construction site in this photograph taken on May 26, 1927. Scaffolding from the work crew is in front of the unfinished building in the background.

From left to right, Alva D. Myers, A.T. Mickle and Chester R. Bunker stand next to Scotty's shack during a 1927 visit. The three men were touring the area after Bunker, a con artist, purchased Death Valley Mines, Inc. Note that "Death Valley Scotty" and a drawing of a skull and crossbones are written on the board between Myers and Mickle. Twenty years earlier, Myers, the founder of Goldfield, Nevada, accused Scotty of stealing high-grade ore from Goldfield mines, then claiming it came from his own secret mine to con investors, including Albert Johnson. Scotty became aggressive with Myers, attempting to prop up his fading reputation with Johnson, but Myers gave Scotty a black eye, both literally and figuratively.

Three members of the castle construction crew stand next to their flatbed truck in October 1928. The two men on the right are supporting one of the thousands of cement fence posts that surround the castle grounds. This gives a good perspective of how large the posts actually are.

This gravel-and-sand gathering building is located in Grapevine Canyon below the castle itself. The 30,000 cement fence posts used by Scotty and Albert M. Johnson to surround the castle complex were made in this building. The snow-covered mountains in the background are far more distant than they appear and are actually located on the far side of Death Valley.

During construction of the castle, Albert Johnson hired the Bullfrog Goldfield Railroad to bring building supplies to Bonnie Claire, the station closest to the castle. When the railroad ceased operations in January 1928, Johnson promptly bought 100,000 railroad ties from the abandoned road for use as firewood. Here, some of these ties are being hauled to "Tie Canyon" in back of the castle.

The caption on this photograph reads, "This is Tie Canyon in back of the Castle. Johnson and Scotty bought these ties from the Tonopah and Tidewater Railroad for $1500 and spent $25,000 to have them hauled in." The ties were actually purchased from the Bullfrog Goldfield Railroad. It has been said that there were enough ties to keep all of the castle's fireplaces going for over 100 years. (Murray.)

Scotty's Castle is still under construction as seen in the background to the left in this photograph, taken on October 2, 1928. In the foreground, workers are making cement posts in place for the fence that will eventually surround the grounds. The back of the photograph noted that the total cost of the fence was $24,500.

The grounds and buildings of the castle are shown in this photograph. Written on the back of the image is the following: "Shows the general topography., January 31, 1930." The faint pencil notation at the top of the photograph reads, "A [sic] Indian Camp," with a line drawn down to the location of the Indian camp. The camp was where a number of the Indian workers lived during the construction of the castle.

When Death Valley's borax mines started closing, the Panamint Shoshone Indians that were living and working in Death Valley started to work for Albert Johnson to help build Scotty's Castle. A hatless Death Valley Scotty (in the white shirt and tie) and two unidentified men to the left of the dog (center) pose with some of these Indians.

This snapshot photograph shows an Indian construction worker piling up logs at the castle during its construction. These logs would have been used to fuel the fireplaces at the castle during the winter. A portion of Scotty's car can be seen on the right. The photograph was taken on December 31, 1928.

This is thought to be the only known photograph taken of Death Valley Scotty's wife, Josephine, who he called "Jack," while she was at the castle. This photograph, taken in March 1928, shows the castle being built, as evidenced by the construction equipment and the large excavated hole. Scotty had a very tempestuous relationship with Jack, and they lived most of their lives apart.

Scotty's Castle was an active construction site when this photograph was taken in 1928. The castle and its grounds were not open to the public at the time this image was captured, so it was taken at a distance during another trip to the area made by mining men A.D. Myers, A.T. Mickle, and Chester R. Bunker.

The construction at Scotty's Castle is easily visible in this photograph. The photograph was taken in 1928 by Warden Woolard (or at least he took credit for it), an editor of the old *Los Angeles Examiner* newspaper and great friend of Scotty.

This photograph is captioned "the Clock Tower" and was taken during construction of the castle on November 8, 1928. The view was actually taken from the clock tower looking east from its balcony. The clock tower, sometimes referred to as the chimes tower, is a separate structure from the main house and the annex.

This photograph of Scotty's Castle was taken in during the winter of 1928–1929 during a lull in the construction due to the heavy snow fall. At this time, Albert Johnson was in the process of listing the furniture and hardware to be placed in various rooms of the castle, as well as the tasks yet to be completed for each room.

This photograph shows the power plant building under construction. The chimes tower is in the background, and the whole construction site is under a blanket of heavy snow. Though undated, this photograph was taken during the 1928–1929 winter snowstorm that hit the castle area.

Three workers and a supervisor (standing in the center) are amidst what appears to be a forest of stands of rebar during construction of the castle. The panels for the innovative solar water heater can be seen on the ground to the right. The photograph was taken on January 31, 1930.

This photograph gives a good idea of the magnitude of the remodel project and the amount of material required. The notation written on the back of the photograph says, "Steel in roof of cross tunnel," and the image is dated February 5, 1930.

This photograph shows one of the original three wooden-sided canvas tents at the Upper Vine during the construction of the castle. The earliest accommodations at the Upper Vine Ranch consisted of the wooden Steininger cabin, which Scotty eventually moved into, and three wooden-sided canvas tents—one used first for Scotty and later as a cookshack and two that housed the Johnsons.

This photograph was taken on March 25, 1930 and bears the notation "Putting in tunnel to clock tower." When remodeling the castle from the first stucco buildings, the castle workmen excavated a basement from which several hundred feet of tunnels extended to various outbuildings, including the clock tower. This tunnel provided access to the water, sewer, and electric lines.

This snapshot photograph has the handwritten note "Landed on Dry Lake between Bonnie Claire and the Castle" on the back. Bonnie Claire was the closest railhead to the castle during construction and was instrumental in getting supplies and materials for its building. Though the man in the white shirt bears a resemblance to Scotty, he is not wearing a hat or tie, which Scotty habitually wore.

Palm trees are associated with Death Valley and Scotty's Castle, but they are not native. This photograph is marked with the following: "Taking in one of the two full grown palms they trucked all the way from L.A. by way of Las Vegas—about 500 miles." It was taken on March 19, 1930, during the construction of Scotty's Castle.

Dietzmann's Iron Craft Works made the large wrought iron planters in the castle that have been located at various times in the central patio courtyard, the lanai, and the second-floor veranda. This identical planter was a part of Dietzmann's overstock, and the German immigrant ironworker who made it was allowed to purchase it and take it home.

This is a business card for Dietzmann's Iron Craft Works, which was located in Los Angeles. On the back of the card, written in pencil, is the following: "Back photo of Death Valley Scotty's stock." Julius Dietzmann was known to have done much ornamental hand wrought iron work at Scotty's Castle.

The 1941 guidebook *Death Valley Scotty's Castle*, written by Bessie Johnson, describes this weather vane as "Weather vane on one of Castle towers—Scotty frying bacon." The castle's consulting architect, Alexander MacNeilledge, designed the wrought iron weather vanes for the castle. He used various designs depicting vignettes of Death Valley Scotty in the desert.

This photograph is a close-up of the castle's wrought iron weather vane showing Death Valley Scotty walking behind his pack mule on a prospecting trip in Death Valley. In addition to Alexander MacNeilledge's designs, Scotty's Castle designer Martin de Dubovay prepared the drawings for the castle weather vanes.

The ubiquitous "S" and "J" initials are found many places both inside the castle and outside throughout the grounds. Hundreds of concrete posts that fence the castle grounds are marked S and J. The cattle on the Death Valley Ranch were branded with the S and J brand. Shown at left is a screen on one of the basement windows. The photograph below shows the Scotty and Johnson branding iron, commissioned especially for the castle by Albert Johnson. Many of the design elements at Scotty's Castle also bore the S and J initials, including the cement fence posts.

When renovations and restorations of the castle are necessary, every effort is made to keep as much of the design and original elements unchanged. In 2013, this fence post was made, and the original S and J markings were used in keeping with the theme of Death Valley Ranch.

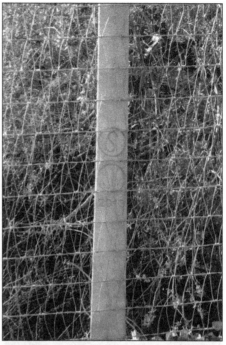

Albert and Bessie Johnson designed their china place settings specifically for the castle. In keeping with the S and J motif used throughout the castle and grounds, all the china was marked "J DVR S," which stood for Johnson, Death Valley Ranch, and Scotty.

Scotty's Castle contains an elaborately tiled kitchen with many conveniences. The large tiled-floor kitchen has a sink that is surrounded by colorful and elaborate Spanish-style tile work. The colorful tiles also cover the walls, enclosing the gas range and oven that are designed to resemble a hearth and the circular area around the false water well (which was actually a trash bin).

One of the stories that Death Valley Scotty used to tell visitors was that he built the castle over his secret gold mine. He pointed out this pulley-driven device in the kitchen and declared he would use it to haul up gold ore from the mine whenever he needed money. In reality, this was used for trash.

The castle's sundial is located on the exterior wall of the upper music room. It can be seen while inside the castle, as it is visible from the window in Albert Johnson's bedroom on the second floor of the Johnson suite. Note the double-sided Janus head above the gnomon.

This photograph shows the fountain in the great living hall. It was taken during the construction of the castle. It is made of native rocks, over which a musical flow of water trickles to the tiled pool below. (Photograph by Warden Woolard.)

This photograph shows only a small portion of the great living hall. The fireplace is to the right, and the upstairs balcony is at top center, just to the left up a staircase. Death Valley Scotty's room (though he never stayed in it) is to the right of the fireplace. The furnishings have handmade wrought iron work and a strong Spanish influence.

The solarium was located on the first floor. It was designed as a pentagonal room with large windows. The design was such that it allowed light in to provide a bright, secluded spot for rest, reading, and relaxation during the sunny daylight hours.

The solarium boasted hand-blocked Spanish linen drapes, which covered the windows when the light proved to be too bright. The drapes are hanging from ornate iron curtain rods that were designed especially for the room and were handmade by specialized craftsmen.

Albert Johnson had the structures at Lower Vine Ranch built partly as a residence for Scotty and partly to lock up water rights near the castle. Scotty lived in this modest four-room house made out of redwood. It had a bedroom, kitchen, dining room, store room, and bath. The house did not have electricity but did have running water and a toilet.

Contrary to what many people believed, Scotty's "shack" at the Lower Vine Ranch was a comfortable four-room cabin. This photograph shows the new, state-of-the-art stove and hot water heater in the Lower Vine kitchen for Scotty's use. Shown here in 2006, the stove still appeared to be serviceable.

Scotty's redwood ranch house at Lower Vine did have running water and a toilet. Shown here is the bathroom sink and commode. Scotty moved the bathtub outside and could often be found sitting in a tub full of water in his long johns.

Death Valley Scotty spent much of his time at the Lower Vine Ranch. Here, Scotty is shown holding one of his mules, who is drinking water from a claw-foot bathtub in the corral. The tub can still be seen today if one takes the seldom-offered walking tour of Lower Vine Ranch.

Indians are working on the fence at Scotty's Lower Vine Ranch. There are extensive records of Indians working on the castle from 1925 to 1931, and this photograph dates from that same time. Pete Cherooty was responsible for lining up the posts, and a Mr. Maxfield was the supervisor.

Scotty is with his beloved mules in the Lower Vine Ranch corrals. The corral system on the Lower Vine Ranch was completed in stages. The yard furthest from the house was completed in 1927. The posts and top rail were of wood, with four strings of barbed wire. A circular training area was added to the feeding area by 1931.

This open-air, ramada-covered structure has a simple tin roof and stick frame. It served as the blacksmith shop and was the last structure added to the building complex in 1931. At the same time, an additional corral was added on the mesa above the residence at Lower Vine Ranch, which stored an additional supply of hay.

The feed shed at Lower Vine Ranch was completed by 1931 during the last phase of the construction of the corrals. It was located just to the east in the yard farthest from the Lower Vine Ranch house.

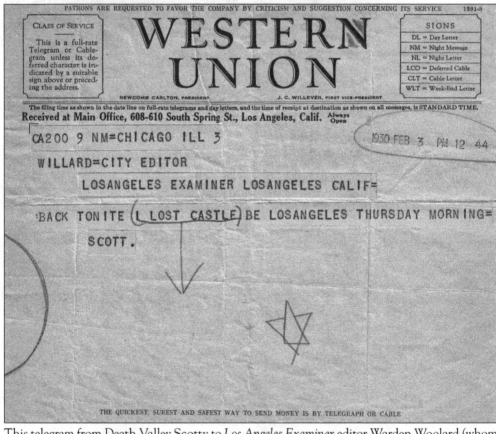

This telegram from Death Valley Scotty to *Los Angeles Examiner* editor Warden Woolard (whom Scotty always called "Willard") states, "I lost Castle" on February 3, 1930. This telegram was sent by Scotty at the beginning of the long-running controversy that started when a US government survey revealed that Albert Johnson did not own the land on which the castle was being built.

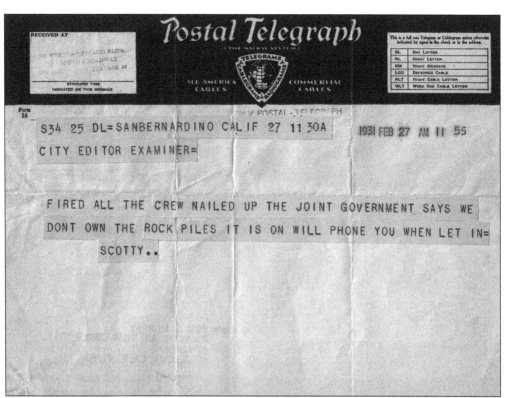

Form 16

S34 25 DL=SANBERNARDINO CALIF 27 11 30A   1931 FEB 27 AM 11 55

CITY EDITOR EXAMINER=

FIRED ALL THE CREW NAILED UP THE JOINT GOVERNMENT SAYS WE DONT OWN THE ROCK PILES IT IS ON WILL PHONE YOU WHEN LET IN=

SCOTTY..

This February 27, 1931, telegram from Scotty to the city editor of the *Los Angeles Examiner* gives Scotty's version of the controversy with the US government over the dispute as to the exact location of Scotty's Castle: "Fired all the crew. Nailed up the Joint. Government says we don't own the rock piles it is on. Will phone you when let in. Scotty."

Chicago, Ill., May 12, 1933.

Dear Scott:

I was very glad to get your last two letters and to know how everything was coming along with you.

You certainly had a hard time laying out two days at Saratoga Springs waiting for the water to go down.

I am sorry you are having trouble with your tooth. If it is decayed or abscessed you had better have it pulled out before it affects your general health.

It is too bad you got your shoulder laid up from shoeing one of the mules. How is it coming along?

Arentz introduced a bill in the last Congress to give you and me the right to secure title to the Upper and Lower Grapevine Ranches, but the time was so short before the expiration of Congress that it did not pass. I have a letter from Congressman Englebright, who is a Member of Congress from the Second District of California, which is the district in which Death Valley is located, that he is all ready to introduce a bill in this Congress, or if not in this one in the next, to the same end that we may get title to the Upper and Lower Grapevine Ranches. This present congress is a special session called by the President to get his special bills through, and it may be that they will not allow any routine bills such as ours to be introduced at this congress. If not, Mr. Englebright is going to try and introduce it at the next.

I have written Governor Scrugham and he has replied, saying he would be glad to do anything he could to help us when the bill comes up. He has also written me a letter which I received today, in which he states that he plans to have a small party of Congressmen accompany him to Nevada on an exploration trip and asking if it would be convenient for us to let them visit the Castle. I wrote him that there was no one there but a watchman but that you and I would be glad to extend such hospitality as we had

Albert Johnson writes to Scotty on May 12, 1933, giving Scotty an update on the bills in Congress that would allow Scotty and Johnson the right to secure the title to the Upper and Lower Vine Ranches. The letter mentions the politicians Johnson has enlisted to help, including Congressman Samuel S. Arentz, Congressman Harry Lane Englebright, and Gov. James G. Scrugham.

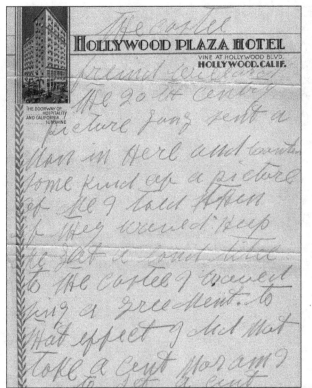

This first page of a letter written by Death Valley Scotty on January 3, 1935, enumerates Scotty's efforts to help Johnson with the disputed title issues for the castle. It says, "The 20th Century picture gang sent a man in here and wanted some kind of a picture of me. I told them if they would help me get a land title to the castel [sic] I would sign an agreement to that effect."

Scotty stands on a rail, looking out at the unfinished swimming pool, in this photograph taken September 26, 1936. The windows seen just below the rail on the left side of the pool allowed visitors in the basement to observe the swimmers under water. A telescope can be seen on the veranda, and the wrought iron weather vane with Scotty and his burro was completed at this time and is in place at the top of the tower.

Two

ALBERT AND BESSIE JOHNSON

Albert Johnson was the builder and owner of Scotty's Castle. He was also the source of Death Valley Scotty's wealth and supported Scotty's lifestyle. Like Scotty, Johnson was born in Ohio in 1872. He earned a mining engineering degree from Cornell University, where he met and married a classmate, Bessilyn M. Penniman, from California. Johnson went into business with his father, a prominent banker and industrialist. He was with his father in Colorado inspecting a mining property when they were in a bad train accident that killed his father and broke Johnson's back, which plagued his health for the remainder of his life.

Unable to continue in the mining business, he bought an insurance company. In 1904, Johnson met Death Valley Scotty, who promptly convinced Johnson to grubstake him in exchange for an interest in any mines located in Death Valley by Scotty. Thus, Johnson became one of Scotty's early con victims by investing in Scotty's nonexistent mining ventures. Unlike others who were duped by Scotty, Johnson and Scotty became lifelong friends. Johnson provided Scotty with plenty of money and was happy to sit on the sidelines and be amused by Scotty's antics.

The real dividends came when Johnson would accompany Scotty to Death Valley and noticed his chronic pain abating and his health improving while he was having a great time. The fact that Scotty did not have a mine did not concern Johnson, who was content to be "repaid in laughs."

Johnson enjoyed coming to Death Valley more and more often with his wife, Bessie. After several visits, Bessie required a nice place to stay. As a result, Johnson spent between $2 million and $3 million to build his Death Valley Ranch, a vacation home that evolved into the complex of buildings now known as Scotty's Castle.

The caption written on the back of this photograph is typical of how the public viewed Scotty, Johnson, and the castle: "Albert Mussey Johnson, partner of Death Valley Scotty, and his wife, Bessie Morris Penniman Johnson, shown here, conduct evangelistic services in Scotty's $2,381,000 mystery Castle which is ringed by ghost cities of a bonanza past."

Alfred MacArthur (left) was one of Albert Johnson's top aides in his Chicago insurance business. In 1908, Johnson sent MacArthur to Death Valley to live with Scotty for several months with the hope that Scotty would show Alfred his secret gold mine. Bill Keys (right) was a scout for Death Valley Scotty in the early days and played a big part in the battle of Wingate Pass, in which Scotty's brother Warner was severely wounded.

After Scotty made his "public confession" that his secret gold mine was a big hoax, Julian Gerard, his first grubstaker, did not believe Scotty's protestations. So, in 1940, Gerard filed suit in federal court in Los Angeles against Scotty, seeking a share of Scotty's wealth in return for the 1907 grubstake. A smiling Scotty in court shakes hands with Gerard while Albert Johnson (the real source of Scotty's wealth) looks on.

Death Valley Scotty (left) and Albert Johnson (right) stand on Locomotive No. 3939. Both men are waving their hats as if in response to the crowd after Scotty's record-setting run, though this locomotive was not used in that historic trip. This photograph was taken on May 23, 1938.

Death Valley Scotty (center, wearing a white shirt and hat) and Albert Johnson (right, wearing a hat, coat, and boots) stand in the middle of the mule corral on their ranch in Grapevine Canyon. The photograph was taken on December 18, 1928, during the construction of the castle.

Death Valley Scotty butchers a hog on his Lower Vine Ranch, a few miles from the castle. Albert Johnson stands on the far right. Although Scotty was a blowhard con man to some people, the reality was much more complex. During the last part of the 19th century, Scotty was a cowboy with *Buffalo Bill's Wild West Show* for about 10 years before he achieved national fame in Death Valley. (NPS.)

Scotty and his dog are going over the plans for the castle with Albert Johnson. The castle was originally conceived as a two-story stucco house, but the plans for the house kept changing until the Spanish-influenced mansion began construction in 1925. Albert Johnson was a Chicago insurance executive that wanted to improve the existing ranch buildings so that when his wife, Bessie, would visit Death Valley, she could stay in comfort.

Albert Johnson (left) poses for a photograph standing next to Death Valley Scotty (right) near the arch at the castle. Johnson looks quite dapper, wearing his long leather riding boots as well as a custom suit. As author and historian Bourke Lee wrote, "Walter Scott brought mystery, romance, and adventure, actively into the life of his partner."

Albert Johnson (left) and Death Valley Scotty (right) are closely examining the reading on gold scales. The photograph appears to be taken in an assay office, most likely the one built and funded by Johnson and located in the large garage on the castle grounds.

During the title troubles for the castle, Scotty wrote to the *Los Angeles Examiner* (spelling corrected), "I would like to get title to Castle. I have not seen Johnson nor Mabel [Scotty's name for Bessie Johnson] since I saw you. He told me, as I told you, he would deed his half over to me, when he got back from Chicago . . . he has been gone 11 months. Now that is that."

This photograph, taken on January 15, 1937, exemplifies the relationship between Death Valley Scotty and Albert M. Johnson, who was both Scotty's close friend and his source of funds. Scotty's primary role for Johnson was providing entertainment and laughter, both of which he succeeded at admirably.

Pictured from left to right, Albert Johnson, an unidentified man in a white shirt and tie, Bessie Johnson, Death Valley Scotty, and an unidentified printer examine newspaper printing plates in what appears to be the castle basement.

Albert Johnson is at the dinner table. The caption on the back of this photograph reads, "Johnson at the Castle carving a Thanksgiving turkey. Scotty was usually at the other end of the table carving one too and was continually exploding with a constant stream of Scotty stories to entertain their guests."

Albert Johnson is shown sitting down next to three women in front of a car in the Death Valley desert near Scotty's Castle. The woman on the far right can be seen holding a Kodak camera, which was popular with tourists of the day.

Bessie Johnson is shown dressed to preach in the Chicago Gospel Tabernacle. Comparatively, little is known about Bessie, who was an enigmatic figure compared to both her husband, Albert, and Death Valley Scotty. Some acquaintances described her as a disagreeable person, and others admired and respected her.

Death Valley Scotty (left) and Albert Johnson (right) gaze into Ubehebe Crater, located not too far from Scotty's Castle. A very shrewd businessman, Johnson tried to obtain title to as much of the surrounding acreage to his castle as he could. In addition to outright purchase, Johnson and his team of lawyers would acquire land titles through possession of water rights and mining rights. Ultimately, Johnson was ultimately very successful, owning over 1.5 million acres.

Albert Johnson cuts quite a majestic figure on his horse in this snapshot taken in December 1928. Johnson's physical appearance was quite a contrast to Bessie's. Albert was extremely tall, over six feet five inches, while Bessie was very short, less than five feet tall.

This photograph of Albert Johnson (center) and Death Valley Scotty (right) was taken at the Lower Vine Ranch. The image bears the caption "Johnson and Scotty shows unknown visitor the corrals." This candid view shows a moment of levity with Johnson and the unidentified visitor laughing out loud. Scotty has a deadpan expression, probably after having told a tall tale.

The Johnsons' bedroom suite is located on the second floor of the main castle building. As can be expected, when the Johnsons were staying there, tours would occasionally bypass the suite out of respect for the Johnsons' privacy. It was originally designed as Albert Johnson's bedroom and sitting room. The personal items in this photograph are laid out in anticipation of a tour.

Albert Johnson purchased this Welte-Mignon player piano from a New York showroom. It sits in the corner of the first-floor music room. The small 25-note keyboard to the left of the piano is wired to play any song on the Deagan chimes in the tall clock tower. The Johnsons had musical instruments in several places in the castle, although they did not themselves play.

This is one of the many photographs of Scotty (center) posing with a movie star, although this time, Albert Johnson (far left) is in the image as well with Scotty and William S. Hart (second from right). They are surrounded by nurses. This image was captured in an unidentified location.

This 1939 photograph is titled "Pair to Wed at Death Valley Scotty's Castle." Albert Johnson is in between Joseph Choate and Dorothy Drew, who were married at the castle. Death Valley Scotty was the best man, and Johnson gave the bride away. Nearly 100 guests attended.

Although Albert Johnson (left) and Death Valley Scotty (right) were very close friends (even dressing alike on occasion, as in this photograph), the feelings between Bessie Johnson and Scotty are unclear. Some say that Scotty did not like Bessie, whom he called "Mabel," and that she, in turn, barely tolerated him; however, when she mentioned Scotty in her manuscript, she called him "a fine, great-hearted man."

Albert Johnson set up the Gospel Foundation of California in 1946 in order to facilitate the transfer of the castle on his death. He requested that they keep the castle open to the public and that they take care of Scotty until his death.

Albert and Bessie Johnson pose for a picture in front of their Hollywood home with some of their influential friends. This photograph was taken shortly before Bessie's death in 1943. Standing from left to right are L.D. Hotchkiss (editor of the *Los Angeles Times*), Louise Quitsch (missionary), Vera Hotchkiss, Bessie Johnson, and Albert Johnson.

During the Depression, Johnson's National Life Insurance Company went into receivership. Albert and Bessie were still well off but not nearly as wealthy as they once were. In 1933, they bought this large house on Franklin Avenue in Hollywood, California, where they lived in semi-retirement. (Murray.)

The third section of Albert Johnson's will, dated May 29, 1947, begins at the bottom of the first page and reads, "I give, devise and bequeath unto the Gospel Foundation of California, a religious and charitable corporation . . . all of the residue of my estate." The fourth section named Mary Liddecoat as a joint executor. Johnson died in January 1948, and this will was admitted to probate on February 6, 1948.

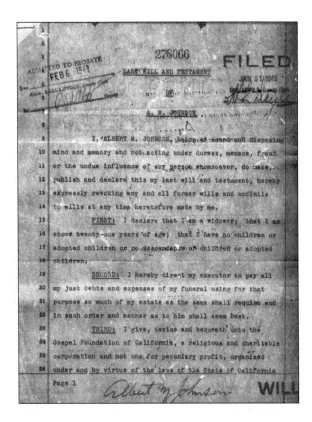

Johnson Will Omits 'Scotty'

Feb 7, 1948

Without opposition, the will of Albert Mussey Johnson, retired insurance executive who "grubstaked" Death Valley Scotty for several decades, was admitted to probate in Superior Court yesterday.

Dated May 29, 1947, the document left an estate of about $50,000 to the Gospel Foundation of California, a religious group.

Before death, Johnson had given most of his large fortune to the Foundation, including the $2,000,000 Death Valley Scotty castle, his local home and securities.

No mention of Scotty, whose real name is Walter E. Scott, was made in the will. But directors of the Foundation said he would be permitted to live in a bungalow at the castle, which will be operated as a hotel.

Even though Albert Johnson was a very close fried with Death Valley Scotty for over 40 years, Johnson did not specifically provide for him in his will. Even this was deemed newsworthy, as shown in this short article from the *Los Angeles Herald* on February 7, 1948. However, Johnson did request that the Gospel Foundation of California take care of Scotty.

Scotty (left) and the castle's manager, Henry Ringe (right), pose for a picture next to a car at the castle on February 15, 1948. According to Scotty, Albert Johnson found a secret cache of over 7,500 ounces of gold dust. Johnson was said to have mentioned this to Ringe, who subsequently confirmed Scotty's story after Johnson's death in 1948.

Joseph Palazzo is intrigued by Albert Johnson's 1914 Packard seven-passenger touring car, which is still on display at the castle. As of 2015, it was located in the stables at the far west end of the castle's complex of buildings.

Three

DEATH VALLEY SCOTTY

Walter Edward Perry Scott, or Death Valley Scotty, was born in Cynthiana, Kentucky, in 1872. He first came to Death Valley in 1885 and worked for the Harmony Borax Works. After leaving the area, he became a cowboy in *Buffalo Bill's Wild West Show* from 1890 to 1902. After a disagreement with Buffalo Bill, Scotty returned to Death Valley. Utilizing the showmanship skills acquired by observing Buffalo Bill's world-class publicity machine, Scotty began to promote the sale of his "mines" in Death Valley. In 1905, when Scotty chartered a train to break the speed record from Los Angeles to Chicago, he became a national celebrity. Scotty was a natural public relations expert who successfully kept his name in the papers for almost 50 years by manipulating the press, including feeding stories and scoops to his good friend Warden Woolard, the city editor of the *Los Angeles Examiner*. Scotty's skill extended to spinning negative stories and lawsuits, which followed him all his life. Scotty also loved to be photographed, particularly in the company of movie stars or pretty women.

Scotty's personal life was not so glamorous. He lived most of his life separated and estranged from his wife, Josephine (whom he called "Jack"), and his son Walter Perry Scott, born in 1914. His son told friends he only saw his father three times in his adult life. Jack sued Scotty for divorce in 1937, asking for $1,000 in monthly support, as well as her community property interest in his mines and other property, including Scotty's Castle. The suit ultimately failed since Scotty did not own any mines or other property.

When Scotty's Castle was constructed, a bedroom was built for Scotty, but he preferred staying first in a cabin at Lower Vine Ranch and later at the small redwood house Albert Johnson built for him there. Upon Johnson's death, the Gospel Foundation of California and Mary Liddecoat took care of Scotty until his death in 1954. He is buried above the castle with his dogs on the hill marked with a cross bearing his name.

Walter E. Scott burst on the national scene in July 1905 when he chartered a train to break the Los Angeles-to-Chicago speed record. This photograph depicts a young Death Valley Scotty in 1905 or 1906. Scotty encouraged photographers to capture his image and was not shy about publicity.

Scotty was a cowboy in *Buffalo Bill's Wild West Show* from 1890 to 1902. Scotty is seen at left sitting on a dark horse with a mostly white face, wearing a white shirt, with his hand touching the brim of his hat.

56

This photograph is of the holdup of the Deadwood Stage during a performance of *Buffalo Bill's Wild West Show*. Death Valley Scotty is identified as the cowboy second from the right, wearing a white shirt and a white hat. (Denver Public Library.)

When Death Valley Scotty first left home, he went to Nevada to join up with his older brothers Warner and Bill. This photograph was taken around 1920 and shows Scotty smoking a pipe while his brother Bill looks on. Both brothers took part in Scotty's staged Battle of Wingate Pass in 1906.

This unpublished photograph shows Santa Fe Railway locomotive No. 442 at Santa Fe's La Grande Station in Los Angeles on July 9, 1905, at the start of Death Valley Scotty's "Scott Special" record-breaking train run from Los Angeles to Chicago. No. 442 was the locomotive that ran the first leg (Los Angeles to Barstow) of the Scott Special.

This card, addressed only "Mr. Walter Scott, Chicago, Ill.," was mailed in Los Angeles on July 10, 1905, at the start of Death Valley Scotty's record train run. Evidently the sender thought Scotty was so well known that the Chicago Post Office should be able to track him down to deliver it without any additional details as to where in Chicago Scotty could be found.

In this unusual 1905 photograph, Scotty is not wearing his typical white shirt, and he is using a leash to hold his dog. Scotty is shown standing with dignitaries in Chicago after his arrival at the Dearborn Station in Chicago, setting a new speed record from Los Angeles to Chicago in 44 hours and 54 minutes.

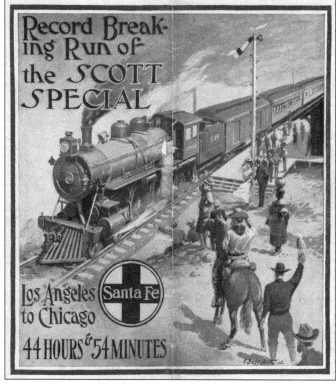

As soon as Death Valley Scotty broke the Los Angeles-to-Chicago speed record on the Scott Special, the Santa Fe Railway published this 1905 promotional pamphlet. It was one of the first publications to cash in on Death Valley Scotty's rise to national prominence. It gives all of the details of the trip, including photographs of the engines and engineers, timetables, maps, elevations, and a detailed analysis.

Daniel E. Owen, Bill Keys, and Warner Scott (Scotty's brother) were part of an elaborate plan by Death Valley Scotty to scare away investors that demanded to see Scotty's (nonexistent) gold mine, in which they invested. The Battle of Wingate Pass was orchestrated by Scotty, but it did not go as planned. Scotty's brother Warner was severely wounded and nearly died when he was accidentally shot in the groin.

Bill Keyes still looks menacing in his later years. Keyes, who was half Cherokee, was an early partner with Death Valley Scotty and an active participant in the Battle of Wingate Pass. Keyes later took part in one of the last gunfights of the West, killing Worth Bagley in 1943, for which he was sent to prison. Keyes's case was taken up by attorney Erle Stanley Gardner, author of the Perry Mason books, and Gardner was ultimately able to secure a pardon for Keyes. (Murray.)

Although Death Valley Scotty lived on the front page for over 50 years, it was not always by his design. The March 3, 1906, *Los Angeles Examiner* gave its entire front page to the Battle of Wingate Pass. Of course, the paper did not know it was Scotty's comrades in arms who ambushed the party and nearly killed Scotty's brother Warner.

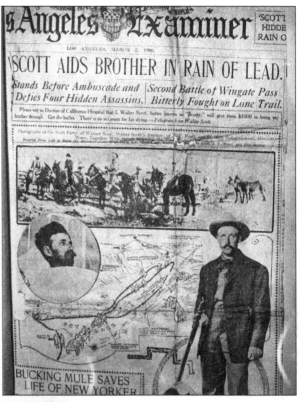

Due to his penchant for semi-legal activities, Death Valley Scotty tried to have friends in the law enforcement community. Here, he sits next to Charles W. "Two Gun Charlie" Benton, a sheriff of nearby Goldfield, Nevada. It was said Benton was "full of guts and thunder and afraid of no man."

61

One of the few times that Scotty was not the main focus of a newspaper story in which he was involved was on July 21, 1911, when he and Wyatt Earp were arrested and jailed in Los Angeles. In an account that was carried in papers throughout the country, Wyatt Earp, Walter Scott, and another man were attempting to swindle J.Y. Peterson, a local real estate man.

This rare photograph shows Death Valley Scotty with a pack train of five mules and his dog leaving the castle on an unknown mission. Whenever this occurred, there was much speculation on the possible explanations for the trips; maybe Scotty was visiting his gold mine, prospecting for more gold, or, as is written on the back of this photograph, "going out to the hills to sing grand opera to his mules."

Death Valley Scotty stands on the far left in this photograph taken in Death Valley in 1906. His wife, Jack Scott, is seated in the wagon that is being drawn by four mules. An unidentified man stands next to the wagon.

Josephine Scott is pictured in this early photograph. Called "Jack" by Scotty, they were married in November 1900. At first, Jack was a part of Scotty's life, but by 1905, they were living apart, with her in Los Angeles and him in Death Valley. Jack was a passenger on the Scott Special but did not enjoy the resultant publicity. They rarely saw each other after that.

Scotty spent most of his life estranged from his wife, Josephine. They were together long enough for Scotty to father a son, Walter Perry Scott, who he rarely saw and seldom mentioned. In this rare photograph, Scotty, Josephine, and their son Walter pose for a picture outside the castle in Death Valley.

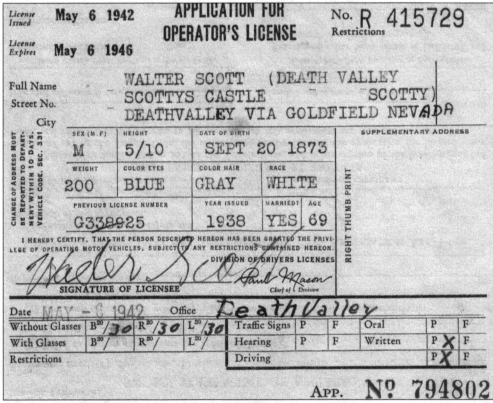

Pictured is Death Valley Scotty's 1942 California driver's license, signed by Scotty. Note his address at Scotty's Castle, Death Valley via Goldfield, Nevada, and that his name "Death Valley Scotty" is listed parenthetically after his given name "Walter Scott." Scotty was 5 feet, 10 inches tall, weighed a sturdy 200 pounds, and had blue eyes.

Death Valley Scotty butchers a hog on his Lower Vine Ranch, a few miles from the castle. He was a proficient cowboy and worked as such on the Death Valley Ranch, as seen in this 1928 photograph.

Scotty entertains an old friend at the castle. Although this photograph bears the caption "Scotty and old friend believed to be a rider in Buffalo Bills Show," it probably is an old Death Valley acquaintance since, on close examination, Scotty is holding a photograph of a group of men standing in front of a Death Valley borax wagon.

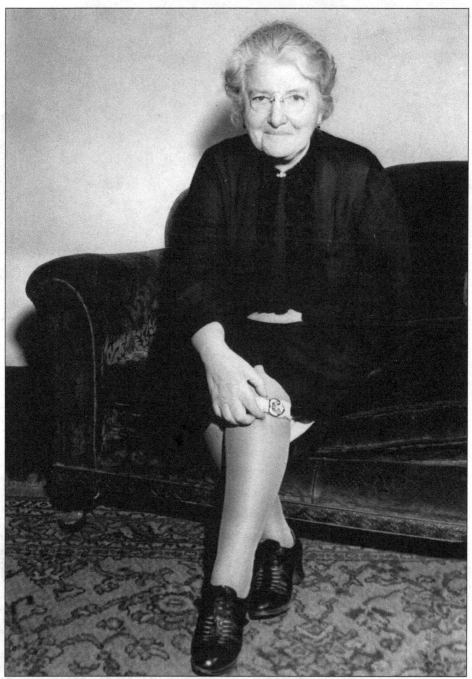

Tired of Scotty's antics and separate life, Josephine filed for divorce in 1937. She put out her own publicity photograph, but Scotty placed his own spin on it, referring to her as his "alleged wife" in the wording for this January 1937 photograph's description: "Although she is suing for separate maintenance of $1,000 monthly from Walter E. "Death Valley" Scotty, famous desert character whom she claims she married in 1900, Mrs. Josephine Scott still wears a sterling silver garter buckle which bears a picture of Scotty. Meanwhile process servers are seeking the millionaire mine owner who has mysteriously disappeared since first filing of his alleged wife's suit."

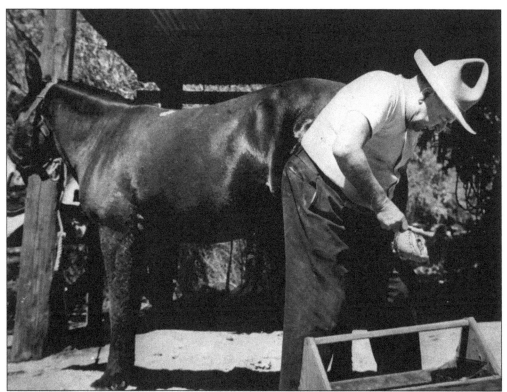

Even in old age, Scotty still performed chores around the ranch. This photograph bears the caption "Death Valley Scotty in his old age shoeing a mule at his ranch on the 'Lower Vine.' One time while Scotty was shoeing a new mule, it kicked and broke Scotty's shoulder."

Death Valley Scotty appeared in federal court in Los Angeles on March 13, 1941, to contest a lawsuit "that may reveal for the first time the source of his mysterious wealth," which he "built a fantastic $2,381,000 desert Castle." Scotty said of his black eye, which is readily apparent in this photograph, that it was a result of a kick his mule Star Dust gave him.

Scotty feeds five of his mules from a metal bucket just outside of the castle near the ranch. Scotty took very good care of his mules, who in turn were devoted to him. This photograph, taken by Los Angeles photographer C.C. Pierce, notes that "they [the mules] returned Scotty's love for him by saving his life several times."

This photograph was taken in 1930 by Cliff Wesselmann and shows Death Valley Scotty talking with his automobile mechanic just outside the main gate of the castle. Three of Scotty's dogs accompany him. Material for the continuing construction of the castle can be seen directly behind Scotty and the mechanic.

Scotty loved animals. Here, Scotty is shown resting in the central patio at the castle with his pet dog, Windy, that accompanied him most of the time. Windy and Scotty's other dogs would "scout" for Scotty in both the city and in the desert, making sure the path was clear and no danger was present. Windy is buried next to Scotty.

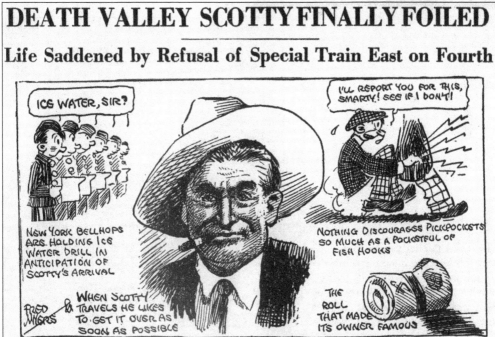

The *Los Angeles Times* ran this cartoon in 1927 when the railroads refused to charter Scotty a train so Scotty could try to break his speed record to Chicago. They reportedly told him, "This is not 1905," and there were too many trains hauling perishable foods that would have to be side-tracked.

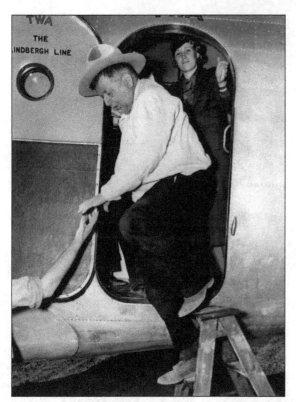

A special flight was made by Trans World Airlines (TWA) to Scotty's Castle on May 27, 1937. Scotty was considering whether to copy his Los Angeles-to-Chicago train record by setting a similar record in an airplane. Here, he is being helped down from the plane after his first airplane flight. Note the terrified look on his face.

The TWA publicity department sent this letter to famed national columnist Walter Winchell, giving him advance notice of Death Valley Scotty trying to set the Los Angeles-to-Chicago air speed record. Note that it was TWA that suggested the record run to Scotty and not the other way around as was commonly reported. Also note that Scotty had to obtain Albert Johnson's permission first.

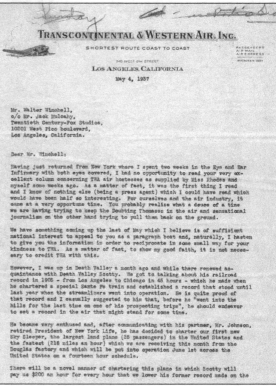

Death Valley Scotty is shown with M. Early flying over Death Valley in a TWA plane in 1937. The caption on the image reads, "Now Scotty is making a trans-continental trip via TWA plane and is willing to 'Bet 'em $200 an hour for every hour they break my record of 32 years ago.'" While Scotty had not lost his flair for showmanship, he had lost color in his face and is smoking a cigarette to try to calm himself.

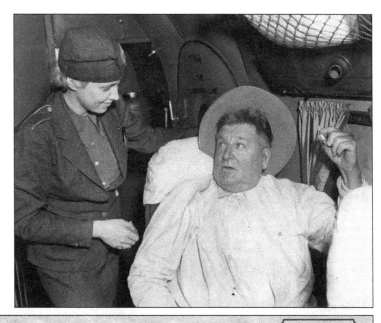

<pre>
CLASS OF SERVICE   WESTERN   SIGNS
This is a full-rate   DL = Day Letter
Telegram or Cable-   NM = Night Message
gram unless its de-   UNION   NL = Night Letter
ferred character is in-   LCO = Deferred Cable
dicated by a suitable   NLT = Cable Night Letter
sign above or preced-   WLT = Week-End Letter
ing the address.
          NEWCOMB CARLTON, PRESIDENT   J. C. WILLEVER, FIRST VICE-PRESIDENT

The filing time as shown in the date line on full-rate telegrams and day letters, and the time of receipt at destination as shown on all messages, is STANDARD TIME.
Received at Main Office, 608-610 South Spring St., Los Angeles, Calif. Always Open

 BY NE 28

      BEATTY NEV 205P JUL 28 1931

 WARDEN WOOLARD

           CITY EDITOR EXAMINER LOSANGELES CALIF

 WIRE RECEIVED WHILE SOBER CANNOT PLACE DR DELAURENCE NEVER WAS

 CONNECTED IN ANY PUBLISHING COMPANY   HE LEFT NOTHING TO ME

 IN WILL WILL SEE YOU ABOUT AUGUST EIGHTH

                              DEATHVALLEY SCOTTY

                                   233P

          WESTERN UNION GIFT ORDERS SOLVE THE PERPLEXING QUESTION OF WHAT TO GIVE
</pre>

Despite the occasional proclamation of Scotty's sobriety by biographers, this telegram from Scotty to *Los Angeles Herald Examiner* city editor Warden Woolard paints a different picture: "Wire received while sober. Cannot place Dr. Delaurence. Never was connected in any publishing company. He left nothing to me in will . . . Death Valley Scotty."

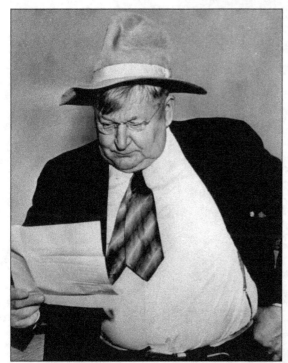

Scotty could be vain and is rarely shown wearing glasses. This publicity photograph was taken on January 25, 1937, and shows Scotty wearing glasses while reading court papers in Arizona; he was waiting for the court to decide on a support suit brought by his wife.

Death Valley Scotty shows off his mules at the castle. The photograph is captioned "Death Valley Scotty loved his mules and bought the best money could buy. One day he showed up at the home of Warden Woolard. When Mrs. Irene Woolard opened the door, Scotty handed her a huge box of candy and said, 'Irene, I know you will like these because my mules do too.' "

The filing time as shown in the date line on full-rate telegrams and day letters, and the time of receipt at destination as shown on all messages, is STANDARD TIME.

Received at Main Office, 608-610 South Spring St., Los Angeles, Calif.   Always Open

MINUTES IN TRANSIT
FULL-RATE | DAY LETTER

3CR OM 38 NL

BEATTY NEV SEP 17 1934

WARDEN WOOLAND

CITY EDITOR EXAMINER LOSA.

I WANT TO TALK TO YOU PERSONALLY BEFORE I MOVE THE MULES LOAD
THERE IS OTHERS FIGHTING TO GET THE STORY TAKE ALL BETS AND GIVE
RACE TRACK ODDS I PROMISED YOU THE STORY YOU WILL GET IT

SCOTT

840A18

In this September 17, 1934, telegram from Scotty to *Los Angeles Herald Examiner* city editor Warden Woolard, Scotty demonstrates his skill as his own press agent. The telegram discusses Scotty moving his mules and fighting to get the story for Woolard, stating, "I promised you the story and you will get it."

Tom G. Murray recalled that one morning he went to Scotty's door at 5:00 a.m., and Scotty was in his long underwear throwing bread to the birds. This photograph, taken by Tom G. Murray on a different occasion also shows Scotty feeding the birds but not so early in the morning and fully dressed.

Scotty is shown relaxing while sitting in a chair outside his bedroom at the castle in between visits from the tourists. This photograph by Tom G. Murray dates a few years earlier than similar images also captured by Murray shortly before Scotty's death. In the later images, Scotty wears tennis shoes, which were more comfortable for his swollen feet.

The cover of this issue of Harry Oliver's *Desert Rat Scrapbook* featured Death Valley Scotty and Scotty's Castle (seen in the background). The lead article was a biography of Death Valley Scotty by Dane Coolidge, an author, novelist, naturalist, and poet. A number of Coolidge's books featured Death Valley Scotty, and his western novel *Snake-Bit Jones* was based on Scotty.

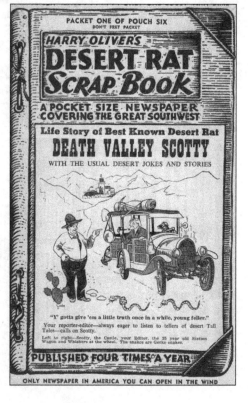

Walter P. Scott is standing with his wife and daughter in front of the door leading to the great hall where Scotty usually entertained his guests. Walter was Scotty's only child. Scotty did not have very much to do with his wife and son and lived alone most of his life. This photograph was taken after Scotty's death. (Murray.)

The front page of the January 6, 1954, *Los Angeles Times* carried a large headline announcing the death of Death Valley Scotty. Although the title and accompanying article states that Scotty died "in the famous Castle that had long been his home," he actually died near Scotty's Junction while being rushed to the hospital in Goldfield.

The caption on the photograph reads, "Death Valley Scotty lies in state in front of the huge fireplace in the great hall of the Castle. The chairs where Johnson and Scotty sat entertaining their guests were roped off. Only the Castle's help and a few friends attended the funeral. It was a quick service because it was feared that the park rangers would not be able to handle the thousands of cars that would jam the narrow roads." Scotty died on January 9, 1954, and is buried with his dog on a hill located just a short walk from the back of the castle.

Scotty's grave is marked by a large cross and a bronze plaque on a hill overlooking the castle. The grave of his beloved dog Windy is to the right next to Scotty's and is marked by the smaller rock pyramid. Shortly before he died, Scotty told a friend "Bury me on the hill it is solid rock. I'll keep forever there." (Murray.)

Four

ENTERTAINMENT AND ENTERTAINERS

The novelty of a large mansion in the middle of a place called Death Valley, the social prominence of the Johnsons, and the publicity-seeking, charismatic, allure, and celebrity of Death Valley Scotty attracted the interest of the rich and famous. In addition, there were friends (and those who wished to be their friends), family, acquaintances, and the adventurous.

Regardless of the relationship to either Albert Johnson, Bessie Johnson, or to Scotty, there were many guests to visit the castle, both invited and those of the drop-in variety. In addition to the well- and lesser-known movie stars, there were also quite a few of Scotty's female "friends" who paid their respects to Scotty and were entertained at his castle.

Death Valley and Death Valley Scotty have had a strong appeal to the entertainment industry for over a century, starting with the 1906 play *The Story of Scotty*, written by Charles A. Taylor, which starred Death Valley Scotty as himself. There was also a 1906 short film *The Secret of Death Valley*. In the 1910s and 1920s, there were many other motion pictures, such as another short, *Death Valley Scotty's Mine*, in which Scotty also starred as himself, and more famously, Eric von Stroheim's *Greed*, which was filmed in Death Valley during the heat of the summer of 1923. There have been well over 100 motion pictures and television shows that have been shot in or near Death Valley or had Death Valley as its subject matter. Scotty's Castle and Death Valley Scotty have both played their parts.

The castle was a filming location for a number of motion pictures, such as the 1982 film *Death Valley*. It was also the inspiration for the fictional castle in the 1942 Charlie Chan mystery *Castle in the Desert*. Death Valley Scotty and Albert Johnson both appeared in the 1944 short film *A Day in Death Valley*. Scotty was the subject of a 1955 episode of the television show *Death Valley Days* and over the years played small parts in a number of motion pictures.

John Barrymore (left) and Death Valley Scotty (right) are pictured in front of Scotty's cabin at Lower Vine Ranch during a weeklong visit by Barrymore during the 1930s. Although Scotty had a bedroom at the castle, he never stayed in it, preferring his "hideaway" cabin a few miles away. It was built by Johnson for Scotty by the same workmen that constructed the castle.

John Barrymore has one arm around Death Valley Scotty and holds a cigarette in his other hand. Scotty holds a rope lariat, or reata, that he used with his mules and horses at the corrals at his Lower Vine Ranch cabin.

Ever since his days with *Buffalo Bill's Wild West Show*, Death Valley Scotty had an affinity for entertainment and entertainers. Scotty capitalized on the national publicity surrounding his record-setting train run from Los Angeles to Chicago by promoting *The Story of Scotty*, written by Charles A. Taylor. Copies of the book were sold at performances of the play of the same name, in which Scotty starred.

After the Scott Special's record-breaking run, the first biographies of Scotty appeared shortly thereafter. The earliest of these was *Mysterious Scott the Monte Christo of Death Valley* by Orin S. Merrill, which was written and published in 1906, as was *The Story of Scotty* by Charles A. Taylor.

Set 25

This is a production still from the 1942 motion picture *Castle in the Desert*, a Charlie Chan mystery starring Sydney Toler. The setting for the movie is a fictional castle located in the Mojave Desert. While the film was not shot in Death Valley, the castle represented was based on Scotty's Castle.

Death Valley Scotty's marketing genius inspired other Death Valley personalities to seek publicity. This rare 1934 photograph shows Charles Ferge, also known as "Seldom Seen Slim," guarding the 80-pound silver bar he found in Owens Lake after it was drained by the Los Angeles Department of Water and Power. Slim was also known to have participated in a movie shoot during the 1920s.

In this candid photograph, Scotty (right) entertains an old friend, Bill Pigue (left), at the castle. They are sitting in the great hall, where most of the castle guests were entertained. Scotty is clearly enjoying himself. "I like this" is written on the back. (Murray.)

The notes with this photograph, dated October 29, 1936, state, "This luxurious living room in Death Valley Scotty's Castle is the scene each Sunday of religious services conducted by the wife of Scotty's close friend, A.M. Johnson. The waterfall in the center background as facaded [sic] with religious stones from the desert." Both Albert and Bessie Johnson were extremely religious.

Death Valley Scotty (wearing white shirt) sits on a mule, and Eva Mudge sits on the mule next to him. The cabin is one of the three original buildings that formed the nucleus for the Johnson's Death Valley Ranch. The three men standing are unidentified.

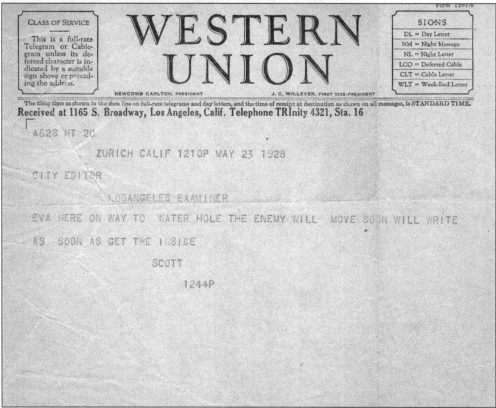

A62S HT 20

ZURICH CALIF 1210P MAY 23 1928

CITY EDITOR

LOSANGELES EXAMINER

EVA HERE ON WAY TO WATER HOLE THE ENEMY WILL MOVE SOON WILL WRITE

AS SOON AS GET THE INSIDE

SCOTT

1244P

Death Valley Scotty sent this telegram on May 23, 1928, to Warden Woolard, the city editor of the *Los Angeles Examiner*, to let him know in advance about actress Eva Mudge coming to the castle for a visit. This was sent during Eva Mudge's famous divorce trial, in which Scotty testified on her behalf.

Though virtually unknown today and largely forgotten toward the end of her life, Scotty's alleged paramour Eva Mudge was a big star in the early years of the 20th century. This song sheet from 1901 featuring Eva Mudge shortly after she left *Buffalo Bill's Wild West Show* was a promotional insert for *Hearst's Chicago American*.

This composite mock-up collage photograph depicts Hans Henry Jorgenson (left) and Death Valley Scotty (right). The image was put together during the divorce trial of Eva Mudge from Jorgensen when Scotty testified on her behalf on May 14, 1928.

This letter was written by Eva Mudge on January 22, 1931, in response to published reports about her romantic involvement with Death Valley Scotty at the castle during her divorce proceedings. She mentions holding Scotty in high esteem, her friendship with Scotty and Johnson, and her time at the Death Valley Ranch. There is a lengthy holograph postscript stating that "any ill reports are utterly untrue."

Death Valley Scotty (who is dressed as a cook) is shown with his dog standing next to "Lord Ely" in this photograph taken on January 10, 1924. Lord Ely was an English exile who took care of Scotty's ranch. Few people were aware that Scotty was an expert cook.

A popular story about Scotty is when a lady visitor to the castle asked, "How do you do your Thanksgiving turkey?" Scotty said, "Lady, you buy the finest turkey and a bottle of good whiskey; every 15 minutes, when you baste the bird, you take a swig of the whiskey. Then, lady, when the whiskey is all gone—who cares about the turkey?!"

Located on the second floor in the annex is the second overnight guest room, which was later known as the Bokhara room during the Gospel Foundation Of California period. This view is of the Italian bed against the north wall of the room. Obscured by shadows is a high, flat headboard with a gold sunburst on top. The short legs of the bed with large pointed gold finials are in the foreground.

Some privileged guests who visited the Johnsons were allowed to spend the night in one of the guest rooms or suites. While not as opulent as the rest of the castle, the rooms were well appointed and tastefully decorated. This guest bathroom is adorned with Spanish tile.

After Albert Johnson purchased a large theater organ, the upper music room was added to the castle on the second floor of the annex at the east end of the hall. The Welte-Mignon theater organ that Johnson purchased was transported and installed at a total cost $50,000 in the 1920s.

This photograph was taken by Tom G. Murray from the veranda at the castle. In it, Death Valley Scotty is shown in a typical pose while entertaining a number of guests around a table in the great hall.

Scotty is shown having makeup being put on him by a pretty movie starlet at the castle for an unknown photo shoot. When the movie director started to give Scotty orders, Scotty told the director to take his crew and "get the hell back where they came from."

This photograph of Scotty with his hands outstretched captures him in a rare appearance in front of a sound camera. Scotty was known to talk a lot with his hands, and from a distance, it looked as though he was using Indian sign language.

Lee---
Memo to Mr. Morgan
1/ 23/ 36

werken -
Zye

This is the Walter Scott situation:

Jack Certok, head of the shorts department at M-G-M, was approached by someone in Scotty's behalf; but Certok, who declines to name the
man he talked to, was not interested in making any short subjects around
Scotty. He did not make an appointment to talk to Scotty at 10 a.m. Friday.
Harry Rapf, the only other shorts authority at M-G-M, knows nothing of the
matter.

Twentieth Century-Fox wants to renew the option on Scott's
story, which expired January 21. William Dover, head of the story department, and Sam Engel, writer and friend of Scotty, are handling the deal there.
The reason nothing was done with the story last year is that Twentieth Century-Fox has Wallace Beery for but one picture a year; therefore, after making
"A Message to Garcia," they can't use him for another year. They want to
star Beery in the Death Valley story, so, according to Harry Brand, if Scotty
will sit tight, Twentieth Century-Fox probably will sign him up again and
eventually get around to filming the story.

But M-G-M, all persons contacted there by Andy Hervey insist,
just isn't interested.

This internal memorandum from January 23, 1936, provides details of the early efforts by Scotty, who approached MGM, to have a movie made about his life. The memo also discusses an option on the story of Scotty's life that was held by 20th Century Fox, which wanted to make the movie with Wallace Beery starring as Scotty.

These contrasting photographs depict the "real" Death Valley Scotty (left) and the version portrayed by Jack Lomas (right). Lomas played Scotty in the 1955 episode of the *Death Valley Days* television show entitled "Death Valley Scotty," which recreated Scotty's record-breaking train run on the Scott Special.

Scotty was an advisor on the 1939 film *Virginia City*. This photograph shows Scotty on the set and is captioned, "Death Valley Scotty, colorful old-time miner and desert an, walked in on a movie location at Calabasas, Calif.,—and stole the show. The movie scene being recorded was one which, in real life, was quite familiar to him. Here is Scotty 'gabbing' with movie actor Alan Hale. 'Them swingin' doors do look mighty invitin' Scotty remarked."

Death Valley Scotty is on the movie set of an unidentified movie. Scotty served as an advisor on a number of motion pictures for Hollywood. Here, Scotty shakes hands with the leading lady as the cameraman and crew look on.

Death Valley Scotty is on a movie set in front of a sign stating, "Last Chance Fill Up Here." Though both the location and film are unknown, the sign was presumably for a gas station located in Death Valley or possibly even the gas station at Scotty's castle itself.

This photograph shows Death Valley Scotty (left), Nevada governor Fred B. Balzar (center), and humorist Will Rogers (eating a hot dog). Will Rogers was said to have admired Scotty for his humor and was Scotty's overnight guest at the castle in 1932. The room where Rogers slept was near the music room and was renamed the Will Rogers room.

The 1982 movie *Death Valley* was promoted as the only movie devoted entirely to the wild beauty that Death Valley so uniquely has to offer. The film was also promoted as "a nightmarish journey into terror." In this photograph, Billy (played by Peter Billingsley) is at the gate of Scotty's Castle and is frantically trying to escape his tormentors.

Catherine Hicks and Peter Billingsley are on the grounds of Scotty's Castle, as can be seen in this photograph of a scene from the 1982 movie *Death Valley*, where Sally (Hicks) is pleased that Billy (Billingsley) is finally beginning to enjoy the trip to Death Valley.

Johnny Shoshone displays a large rattlesnake used in a movie filmed in Death Valley called *Fangs of Death Valley*. Shoshone claimed to have seen the first white men enter Death Valley in 1849. The film was directed by Tom Griffith and starred Pauline Holden and Jack Allman. It was released in 1932 by Principal Distribution Corp.

Never to shy to promote himself, Death Valley Scotty embarked on a personal publicity campaign in the 1930s where he would stage photo opportunities with the motion picture stars of the day. Here, Scotty pretends to give pointers to actors Betty Davis and Leslie Howard at the Warner Bros. Studio in Burbank, California. (Ed Stine.)

Death Valley Scotty (center) poses for this picture while dining with actress Gloria Shea (left) and another pretty girl named Betty near the arch outside at the castle during their visit in 1932. This is a posed photograph with a waiter serving them. It is easy to imagine Scotty regaling them of his early acting days, when he starred in the 1912 film *Death Valley Scotty's Mine*.

This photograph of, from left to right, Betty Gillette, Scotty, and Gloria Shea was taken at the castle in 1932. At this time, Shea had been in several films, mostly uncredited, but had received good reviews for her role in the short film *The Varsity Show*. She later starred in a number of films, notably *Money Means Nothing* (1934) and *The Oil Raider* (1934) before marrying Vice Adm. Robert J. Stroh and retiring.

Scotty called Mrs. Robert Walsh (left) "Freddie" and referred to her as his girlfriend, no doubt as an attempt at flattery. Scotty stands between Freddie and her sister Lillian Pollard as they arrive at the big Hollywood movie premiere for *Lloyds of London* at Carthay Circle Theatre in 1936.

This photograph was taken on June 12, 1936, and bears the note, "Death Valley Scotty, well known character has been photographed from the east to the west coast, but the cameraman caught Scotty in this unusual pose when he . . . is shown dancing with Miss Peggy Page."

T.R. Goodwin, superintendent of Death Valley National Monument (left), and Death Valley Scotty (right) enjoy a moment together at Scotty's Castle. Goodwin was instrumental in taking up the cause of the native Timbisha Indians to prevent their removal from Death Valley Monument during the 1930s. (Murray.)

Written on the back of this photograph is the following: "Scotty in the living room of his fabulous Castle. Although he poked fun at his guests and often called them 'damn emo-grants' he was a great story-teller and the soul of hospitality. He was the last of the great frontiersmen, a man of mystery for whose gold mine many men have died trying to locate it in the vast waste of Death Valley."

Scotty wears a tuxedo while shaking a cocktail at the castle. The caption reads, "Death Valley Scotty drove over one hundred miles to show Helene Eichbaum how 'elegant' he looked in his first tuxedo. He always stopped at Stove Pipe on his way to Los Angeles to say hello to the Eichbaums."

Scotty is at a dressing table with actress Bebe Daniels, looking at themselves in a mirror. The original caption on the back reads, "Bebe Daniels and Death Valley Scotty when Scotty went to Hollywood to do a screen test. He said they'll never show it in any movie houses because, 'I talked the language that mules understand.'"

Death Valley Scotty (left) talks to Mack Sennett (right), possibly on the set for the motion picture *Monkey Business in Africa*, which Sennett directed in 1931. According to Mack Sennett's filmography, Death Valley Scotty was listed in the scenario for the film, but he is not in any of the scenes in the existing prints.

John Barrymore's visit to Scotty's Castle in 1941 drew national attention. In this staged photograph, Scotty shows John Barrymore some of the fine-tooled leather saddles at the castle. It should be noted that these ornate saddles were not the working saddles that Scotty would use.

Death Valley Scotty (left) is pictured with one of his high-profile celebrity friends, Rear Adm. Luke McNamee (right). In April 1931, Death Valley Scotty was the guest of honor at a party tendered aboard the USS *Maryland* and hosted by Rear Admiral McNamee, commander of Battleship Division One. Written on the back of this image is the following: "Scotty now thinks he knows all about the Navy."

Death Valley Scotty was never shy about posing for photographs while entertaining guests at the castle—especially if they were female. If they were young and good looking, so much the better. Here, Death Valley Scotty poses with some friends in the 1930s.

There are conflicting accounts on whether Scotty enjoyed being around children. Whatever his true feelings, he always entertained them and posed for pictures when they were visiting the castle. On this day, Scotty places a tentative hand on the child's leg and has an unreadable expression on his face.

Death Valley Scotty (left) and photographer and author Tom G. Murray (right) relax at the castle during one of their last visits in June 1953. Murray was a friend of Scotty's during the latter part of Scotty's life and loved talking to Scotty while gathering stories about him and Death Valley. Scotty died in January 1954, six months after this photograph was taken.

From left to right, Walter Scott Jr., Cap Gibson, and Tom G. Murray pose for a group photograph in front of the door to the castle. Capt. Ray A. Gibson was known as "the last of the Death Valley teamsters." Gibson came to the Death Valley area around 1899, served as a commissary man, a chainman on the railroad, and a swamper on a freight team. He died in 1976.

Five

TOURISTS AND TOURISM

Ever since Scotty's Castle came into the public eye (largely through the publicity-seeking efforts of Death Valley Scotty), it has become a destination for the curious, even before Death Valley became a national monument in 1933. Visitors would drive up and look around the castle and its grounds to see what all the fuss was about. When the Johnsons were in residence, they would graciously show the visitors around. This became old very fast, and Bessie Johnson instituted informal tours for these drop-in visitors, as she did in 1931 when Eddie Nelson and his family stopped to explore the building and its surroundings.

Ultimately, these informal tours turned into more structured and formal tours, where the visitors would pay a fee and be led by a trained guide. By 1941, the visitors would have an opportunity to purchase a guide book written by Bessie that was followed by the tour guides.

After the death of Albert Johnson in 1948, the Gospel Foundation of California took over ownership and operation of Scotty's Castle, with Mary Liddecoat as its director. The Gospel Foundation of California continued to operate the tours with a changed and revised script. The tours were further reorganized when the National Park Service obtained title to the castle from the Gospel Foundation. The National Park Service increased the number of tours, as well as types of tours offered, and later put the guides in period costumes. When Scotty died in 1954, Liddecoat and the Gospel Foundation closed the buildings at the Lower Vine Ranch to tourists. Starting in 2004, the National Park Service opened up the Lower Vine Ranch buildings and allows limited guided hiking tours during a few weeks each year. These hiking tours are still ongoing today.

Despite the fact that Death Valley Scotty has not been on the scene for over 60 years, as Scotty's Castle approaches its centennial, it still maintains its appeal as a tourist destination, attracting over 100,000 visitors per year.

"Completing Death Valley Castle" is the title of this photograph taken on September 23, 1936. The notation on the back reads, "View of the main buildings of the $2,381,000 structure in Grapevine Canyon near the head of Death Valley. Clock and chimes tower is shown on the left, main buildings in the center, with unfinished swimming pool in center, while other buildings extend half a mile up the canyon."

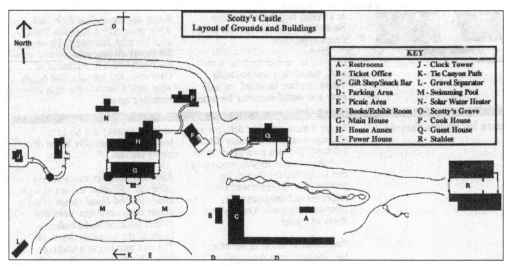

Scotty's Castle
Layout of Grounds and Buildings

KEY	
A - Restrooms	J - Clock Tower
B - Ticket Office	K - Tie Canyon Path
C - Gift Shop/Snack Bar	L - Gravel Separator
D - Parking Area	M - Swimming Pool
E - Picnic Area	N - Solar Water Heater
F - Books/Exhibit Room	O - Scotty's Grave
G - Main House	P - Cook House
H - House Annex	Q - Guest House
I - Power House	R - Stables

This layout of Scotty's Castle grounds and buildings was prepared for the 1995 tourist season. Comparing it with the 1936 "Completing Death Valley Castle" photograph at the top of this page, not too much has changed. The castle itself was never completed, and the use of the buildings from 1936 differs as a result of the facility not housing the Johnsons or tourists.

The road to Scotty's Castle was not paved in March 1932 when this photograph was taken. The photograph is captioned, "Road up the Wash to Scotty's Castle," and was taken by Elbert B. Griffith (1891–1987), the son of Covina, California, pioneer Alfred P. Griffith. Even after Death Valley became a national monument in 1933, auto travel was still a challenge for many years.

This photograph of Scotty's Castle was taken by Eddie Nelson on March 23, 1931, just inside the "big arched gates with very heavy hand forged iron work." Note the concrete fence posts lying on the ground in the left foreground and the stacks of railroad ties from the Bullfrog Goldfield Railroad in the right foreground.

After Eddie Nelson parked his car, his family started to explore the grounds of the Death Valley Ranch. Two other groups were doing the same when Bessie Johnson asked if they would care to go through the buildings. Once inside, in the kitchen, Bessie told one of the "men servants" to be sure to show the visitors everything. During the visit, Albert and Bessie Johnson were present, but Scotty was in Los Angeles.

After visiting the kitchen, the Nelsons "passed on into the dining room. The table was set. I didn't notice the number of places, but not more than one or two. We were shown the dishes from the china closet. They were made to order in Italy and each piece has Mrs. Johnson's and Mr. Scotts name on it."

Some of Scotty's clothes are on display in his bedroom at the castle, which Eddie Nelson noted "opened off the opposite end of the living room and was the most significant room in the building. Large pictures of Buffalo Bill adorned the walls. On his dresser was a picture of the train making the record run to Chicago, with an inserted photograph of the engineer on each run."

In January 1931, Scotty once again made national news when Madaleine Henderson, a University of Nevada coed, was "Lost in Death Valley." Allegedly, her car broke down, and she was rescued by the famous Death Valley Scotty, who found her after she had spent two days and two nights in the desert. Some doubted the story, believing she was Scotty's special guest at the castle for those two days and two nights.

Some doubted the story of Madaleine Henderson and thought she was Scotty's guest at the castle for those two days and two nights in January 1931. According to Eddie Nelson's description of Scotty's bedroom, as seen in March 1931, "Pictures of other notable events in Scotty's career are in abundance, and ranking among the most prominent were several pictures of a girl which Mr. Scott rescued on the desert."

The unfinished swimming pool is in the foreground of this photograph. After finishing his tour of the castle, Eddie Nelson wrote, "Returning to the car we note where the gasoline shovel is working on excavating for a swimming pool to be 300 feet long, with elaborate fountains, and in addition smaller and shallower pools with less elaborate fountains for the children."

106

H.W. "Bob" Eichbaum and his wife, Helene, were responsible for bringing many visitors to Death Valley. They constructed a toll road from Darwin to their Stovepipe Wells resort, which opened up tourism to Death Valley from the west. Death Valley Scotty, shown in front of the castle, signed this photograph to Helene Eichbaum shortly after Bob died in 1932.

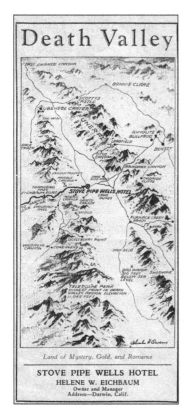

This promotional map was in a brochure given to guests of the Stovepipe Wells Hotel by its owner, Helene Eichbaum. Guests at Stovepipe Wells were encouraged to visit Scotty's Castle, which can be found on the map directly to the north of the Stovepipe Wells Hotel.

This photograph was taken in January 1927 at a meeting in Death Valley of Pacific Coast Borax executives and National Park Service officials to assess the plans for opening Death Valley to tourism. Horace M. Albright sits in the borax wagon, and Steve Mather, the director of the National Park Service, is the man holding a hat directly below him.

PROGRAM

Mt. Whitney - Death Valley Highway Celebration
Oct. 29, 30, 31, 1937

FRIDAY, OCT. 29

Dawn—Indian Runner dips gourd in Lake Tulainyo, 12,865 ft. high.

9:00 a.m.—Children's Sports, Lone Pine. Street North of Hopkins Hardware Store.

1:00 p.m.—Lone Pine: Football, Lone Pine and Bishop High Schools. Rodeo Grounds.

4:30 p.m.—Gourd of water arrives at Whitney Portal, terminus of road whence Pony Express rider starts for Lone Pine.

6:30 p.m.—Water, followed by Chain of Light, arrives at Lone Pine.

7:00 p.m.—Trout Dinner for Governor and visiting officials. Lone Pine.

7:30 p.m.—Lone Pine: Wrestling, Pavilion.

9:00 p.m.—Dancing, Indian orchestra, Lone Pine Union High School. Dancing, Jose Arias Spanish Orchestra, Santa Rosa Hall.

SATURDAY, OCT. 30.

9:00 a.m.—Water starts for Death Valley in Covered Wagon thence transferred to prospector with burro (Death Valley Scotty), thence to stage coach, thence to Twenty Mule Team, and at junction of Highway with narrow-guage railroad, to special train which will carry it to Keeler, sixteen miles distant from Lone Pine, where it will remain overnight. Due at Keeler about 11:30 a.m.

10:00 p.m.—Dancing Lone Pine Jr. V. A. Hall. Old Fashioned Dances, Lone Pine High School. Dancing, Jose Arias Orchestra, Santa Rosa Hall.

SUNDAY, OCT. 31

8:00 a.m.—Outdoor Mass, Lone Pine. Santa Rosa Hall.

9:00 a.m. Protestant Services, Lone Pine. Trinity United Church.

10:00 a.m.—Water leaves Keeler in Lincoln Zephyr auto.

10:30 a.m.—Water arrives at point of Dedication, junction of new Highway and Darwin road. Address by Governor Merriam. Descendant of Manly Party and of Donner Party join hands. Road officially opened by President Roosevelt's flash from Washington, D. C.

12:00 m.—Plane takes water from Panamint Valley over Telescope Peak into Death Valley.

1:00 p.m.—Free Barbecue: Stovepipe Wells, Death Valley. Exhibition Shooting by Capt. Hardy.

2:30 p.m.—Rodeo: Lone Pine.

3:00 p.m.—Reunion of Death Valley Parties, Furnace Creek Inn.

4:00 p.m.—Plane leaves Furnace Creek with water.

4:15 p.m.—Wedding of Waters at Bad Water, 276 feet below sea level.

5:00 p.m.—Signal fires are lit on peaks from Dante's View to Whitney.

In 1937, the Mount Whitney Death Valley Highway bypassed the toll road from Darwin to Panamint Valley and provided tourists a faster route to drive into Death Valley and Scotty's Castle from the west. An elaborate three-day ceremony was held, during which water from Mount Whitney was sent to Badwater in Death Valley using various modes of transportation. Death Valley Scotty carried the water during Saturday's first leg, on the second day of the ceremony.

This panoramic photograph of Scotty's Castle shows much of the castle grounds, including a rear view of the main castle building, the unfinished swimming pool, guest facilities, and other structures. It was taken from the chimes tower. Scotty's apartment (which he did not like to use) is in the bottom left, where his rocking chair can be seen.

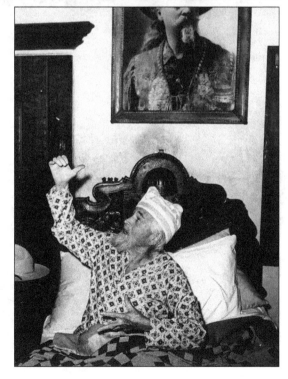

Harry Oliver is shown sleeping in Death Valley Scotty's bed at Scotty's Castle. Oliver was the editor of the *Desert Rat Scrapbook* after having been a set designer in Hollywood and receiving two Academy Award nominations during the late 1920s. The photograph of Buffalo Bill relates to Scotty's early days, when he was a cowboy *in Buffalo Bill's Wild West Show*. (Murray.)

Death Valley
Scotty's Castle

By 1941, formal tours of Scotty's Castle had been organized by Albert and Bessie Johnson for several years. This 73-page book was written by Bessie Johnson in 1941 and was available for purchase by castle visitors. In it, she provides a complete description of the castle and furnishings as given by the castle guides.

This Scotty's Castle guidebook was inscribed by Scotty to William Parker Yaney who writes, "Death Valley Scotty many years ago at his Castle asked me to be his lawyer in a great scheme to net each of us several million . . . I listened, he talked on and that was the end of the matter—for I never returned nor did he mention it further."

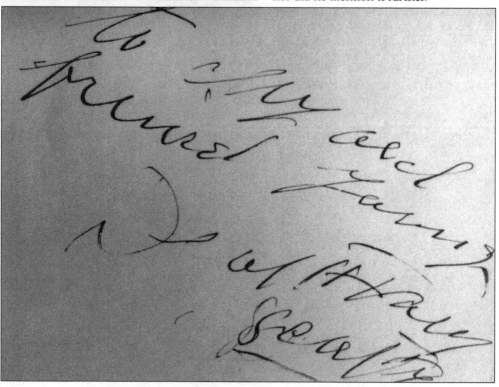

Joseph Palazzo stands next to the ornate wrought iron gate leading to the central patio, located between Scotty's Castle and the annex, where visitors would gather before an organized tour. This view shows the red paved stones on the floor and the weather vane (on top of the tower to the right) of Scotty frying bacon over a campfire.

The first area shown to tourists is the central patio (or courtyard) and garage alcove. The covering for the courtyard consists of eucalyptus poles stretched across its length and width, forming an arbor covered with grapevines. The tiles are red and laid in a herringbone pattern throughout the courtyard. At one time, Albert Johnson parked his car at the west end of the patio by the rear gates.

The large main room in the castle, currently known as the great hall (or great living hall), was called the living room when the Johnsons occupied the castle. Martin de Dubovay designed the overstuffed leather chairs and sofas. On top of the north doorway to the great hall are vases and baskets.

The W.H. Sheidenberger & Sons furniture company crafted the carved gun racks that are located outside the door leading to Scotty's bedroom from the great living hall. Castle tour guides would point out that both Scotty and Albert Johnson were both excellent shots with the rifle and pistol.

There are several block-long corridors winding under Scotty's Castle such as this one, which is barricaded at a dead end. Up until very recently, these corridors were rarely seen by visitors to the castle. The National Park Service now offers tours that include the corridors. Those who knew of their existence often wondered what the purpose of these corridors were. Scotty told them "to keep dry going from building to building when it rains."

The gas pumps and adjacent small building (added later) in front of the castle have been variously used as a private gas station, a public gas station, a ticket booth for the castle tours, and an information kiosk for tourist questions. Gas is no longer available at the castle, but the pumps provide a photo opportunity for this pretty girl named Vivianne and her son.

This snapshot was taken in front of the castle and is marked, "Scotty, Mrs. Ringe and a Waitress and her daughter. Feb. 15, 1948." Gertrude F. Ringe and her husband, Henry, were the managers of Scotty's Castle during the 1940s and 1950s. Gertrude also served as postmaster of the Scotty's Castle Post Office for all six years of its operation.

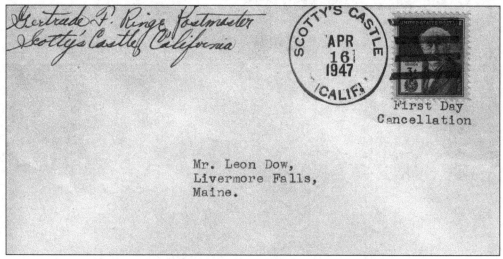

As the number of visitors to Scotty's Castle increased, the US Postal Service opened a post office to serve the large volume of cards being sent by tourists. This envelope was mailed in 1947 on the first day that the Scotty's Castle Post Office was open. It was sent by Gertrude F. Ringe, the postmaster. The post office ceased operations on May 15, 1953.

Some visitors were fortunate enough to have the opportunity to fly over the castle. Several airlines provided this service. This photograph shows how it would look to those who took an airplane to or over the castle in the 1930s.

TWA SERVICES, INC.
Parks Division

Visit
SCOTTY'S CASTLE

IN
DEATH VALLEY
"Scotty's Multimillion Dollar Dream"

General Information Folder

TWA had maintained a relationship with Death Valley since it promoted Scotty's airplane flight over the area in 1937. The Parks Division of TWA Services was the manager of the concessions for the National Park Service when it issued this 1974 information brochure about Scotty's Castle. At this time, TWA Services managed the concessions for the National Park Service at the North Rim of the Grand Canyon, Zion, and Bryce National Parks.

During most of its existence, the castle did not provide lodging accommodations for the general public. This undated photograph was probably taken during the 1930s or 1940s. The sign shown was located at the entrance to Grapevine Canyon. Tourists often photographed the sign itself during the time it was up.

For those tourists making the trip to Scotty's Castle, seeing Death Valley Scotty would be the highlight. If they were fortunate enough to be able to visit with Scotty, a popular way to document that visit was to have a picture taken with him from the balcony in the castle's great hall, like this one from 1948.

The guesthouse (shown covered in snow in 1929), later known as the Hacienda, has 2,800 square feet and 2 two-bedroom suites. After Albert Johnson's death in 1948, when the Gospel Foundation of California managed the castle property and rented out rooms, the guesthouse was divided into four separate units.

The chimes tower at Scotty's Castle is easily recognizable, and its chimes can be heard for many miles. Over the years, tourists have heard a wide selection of music from "Ava Maria" to "Home on the Range" to "I've Been Working on the Railroad," which was one of Death Valley Scotty's favorites. (Murray.)

SCOTTY'S CASTLE

THE CASTLE

In the upper reaches of Death Valley, California, in Grapevine Canyon, stands the fabulous Scotty's Castle. Designed as a luxurious "water-hole" for just two men —it gradually became an overnight spot for prospectors and other wayfarers. Eventually, seasoned world travelers found the Castle—then went on to tell others of the marvels of its architecture, the magnificence of its furnishings and art treasures brought from far corners of the earth.

Scotty's Castle is indeed unique in that it has been opened to visitors in response to a persistent and enthusiastic public demand.

OPEN ALL YEAR

Here is an oasis—in a year-around balmy atmosphere —3000 feet up in Grapevine Canyon.

Summer visitors may come in through California and Nevada points, avoiding any possible intense summer heat in Death Valley basin. (See map on back cover).

THE CASTLE IS AIR-CONDITIONED

Tour the Castle with its treasures—see the Clock Tower, Tie Canyon, ranch house, stables and guest house,— listen to the chimes or the organ, enjoy a "snack"— and be on your way.

Enjoy the grounds free. A leisurely and conducted tour of the spacious and extraordinarily furnished rooms of the Castle and its companion buildings is provided for $1.00 (plus tax) for adults. You will never forget that you have been somewhere and have seen something!!

ACCOMMODATIONS

Breakfast, dinner, snacks served for those who drop by —or stay over night.

LODGING

Accommodations, European, are available in the Hacienda and Rancho. Rates from $6 double. The Castle is not a resort. Accommodations are limited, so reservations are desirable. See your own travel bureau or address:

> **SCOTTY'S CASTLE**
> HEAD OFFICE
> 1462 N. Stanley Ave., Hollywood 46, Calif.
> HO. 5-1223

Deposit for one day's charges should accompany each reservation. Please make checks payable to The Castle. Allow several days time to receive confirmation.

LOCATION

Scotty's Castle is easily reached on oiled roads from all California and Nevada points, as shown on back page map. It is within the Death Valley National Monument as defined by the Federal Government. Oiled roads make quickly reachable such attractions as the Dunes, the Devil's Golf Course, Ubehebe Crater, Dantes View, Furnace Creek Inn and Ranch, Stovepipe Wells, Panamint Springs, Boulder Dam, Rhyolite "ghosttown," Beatty, Goldfield and Tonopah, Mt. Whitney and the entire wonderland of the high Sierra.

AIR CONDITIONED   OPEN ALL YEAR

This Scotty's Castle advertising brochure dates from about 1950. Lodging accommodations are available in both the Hacienda (guesthouse) and Rancho with rates starting at $6 for a double room. In order to make sure guests were not disappointed if they had stayed at the luxury Furnace Creek Inn, the brochure emphasizes the point that "the Castle is not a resort."

This souvenir postcard was purchased at Scotty's Castle on Fourth of July weekend in 1952. It is a typical tourist view and, as was the case in many instances, mailed from a post office outside of the Death Valley National Monument, Tonopah, Nevada, on this occasion, even though the castle had its own post office at this time.

SCOTTY'S CASTLE
Death Valley
California

It is our pleasure to welcome you to the CASTLE. An attendant will meet you in the Court Yard.

The grounds are for your pleasure—there is no charge.

Look around and make yourself at home.

The CASTLE has been opened to the public for the enjoyment of the architectural creations, the art, luxurious furnishings, and the natural beauties which are found here in abundance.

Inside tours of the CASTLE are conducted at intervals. You are assured a most interesting time of it, for $1.00 plus tax. Purchase tickets at COFFEE HOUSE.

Either before or after the inside tour, we suggest that you visit some of the many points of interest OUTSIDE THE CASTLE. These include:

THE DISPLAY of postcard views, souvenirs and novelties in the COFFEE HOUSE.

THE ORIGINAL "CASTLE"

THE HACIENDA, with its charming veranda and cactus garden

THE OLD WESTERN STAGE COACH

THE OLD-TIME "DESERT" PACKARD

THE STABLES

THE CHIMES AND CLOCK TOWER (with view of the canyon).

For your convenience, meals and snacks are served in the COFFEE HOUSE and RANCH HOUSE. There is a selection of choice foods and beverages. Just come as you are.

Single, double, suites and other overnight accommodations are available in the CASTLE and companion buildings. Rates include lodging and breakfast.

Mail your post-cards at our own post-office. They will then bear the post-mark "Scotty's Castle, California."

Gasoline, oil, water, and other motor services available at the gas station.

Listen for the CASTLE bell—it will be the signal that it is tour time for you.

We shall endeavor to make your visit with us one long to be remembered.

SCOTTY'S CASTLE

This Scotty's Castle welcome brochure and information sheet was given to tourists in 1952. As can be seen, at this time, overnight accommodations were available in the castle itself, as well as the guesthouse, and the gas station and post office were also in operation.

This old stagecoach is shown in its previous location outside on the grounds of the castle. It was a featured attraction in the 1952 tourist brochure. Note the cat alongside the coach on the left. As of 2015, it is labeled as a "Concord Western Stage Wagon" and has been moved inside to the stables, which is a covered building.

The last of Scotty's beloved mules, Betty, stands on the hill above the castle near the spot where Scotty is buried by the big cross. She was 49 when this photograph was taken in 1953. Betty lived two more years before joining Scotty in his "Gold Mine in the Sky." (Photograph by Tom G. Murray.)

This candid snapshot of Scotty in the great hall of the castle shows him between two women visitors who are playfully holding him down with a souvenir billy club that Los Angeles sheriff Eugene W. Biscailuz had given to him on a prior occasion.

SCOTTY'S CASTLE

Open All Year—Air Conditioned

Food service: Breakfast, Dinner, Snacks.

RESERVATION AND ACCOMMODATION INFORMATION

LODGING: Rooms and suites available in Hacienda and Rancho. European Plan.

HACIENDA:

	Single or Double	Three
MADRID ROOM Twin beds, tub and shower bath......................	$10	
GRANADA SUITE Large living room, bed divan, twin beds on balcony, lavatory..	12	$15
BARCELONA SUITE Large living room, bed divan, twin beds on balcony, tub and shower bath..........................	14	17
MAJORCA ROOM Twin beds, tub and shower bath......................	10	

RANCHO:

$6.00 single, or double. (Hot and cold water. Shower bath and other facilities nearby.)

$8.00 single, or double. (Hot and cold water. Shower bath en suite.)

When making reservations please include remittance to cover one day's charges. At least five days time should be allowed for confirmation from California points—other points accordingly.

Refund of deposits necessarily conditioned on receipt of notice of cancellation at head office 3 days or more in advance of anticipated arrival date.

Please make checks payable to "The Castle."

All communications and remittances may be mailed to head office:
Scotty's Castle, 1462 No. Stanley Ave., Hollywood 46, California.
Telephone: HOllywood 5-1223

Scotty's Castle was still an overnight tourist destination during the 1955–1956 tourist season, as is evidenced by this advertising brochure and price list. There were a variety of rooms available in all price ranges, as well as other amenities. Note there is air-conditioning and all meals were available at the restaurant. In the 1960s, overnight accommodations were no longer available for tourists.

This artistic photograph bears the florid description, "Death Valley Scotty's Castle, the $2,000,000 Spanish palace in California-Nevada wastelands, where lives the fabulous last great mystery man of the old time west, in isolated Grapevine Canyon. The Castle is 3000 feet above where the canyon enters the hottest, lowest, and deadliest desert in this hemisphere."

Through the decades that Scotty's Castle has been open to tourists, there have been thousands of souvenirs available for purchase to remember the visit. This vintage sterling silver charm reproduces the castle in miniature, measuring just one inch in length, and was sold at the castle during the charm bracelet fad in the late 1950s.

122

Scotty's mule hams it up for the camera. She is in front of the tower outside the music room at Scotty's Castle. This image bears the caption "When Scotty was asked what the mules were for he said 'They haul gas for the trucks—and the trucks haul hay for the mules.' " (Murray.)

This snapshot photograph was taken by a tourist who gave it the title "King of Death Valley and his Castle." It shows Death Valley Scotty standing on a hill in front of the castle. It was taken a month after Albert Johnson died.

This photograph, taken during Scotty's life, depicts the chain-link gates with a "No Hunting" and a "No Trespassing" sign located one half mile from the shack with modern conveniences at Lower Vine Ranch, in which Scotty actually lived. The chain-locked steel gate barred visitors from Scotty's home, located six miles in back of the mountain from the castle. The signs have long since vanished.

Even though Scotty's Castle is associated with the heat of Death Valley, even during a mild spring, the days can be quite cool. This photograph was taken at the Lower Vine Ranch house in March 2006, shortly after it was opened for limited tours and heavy warm clothing was still needed.

This tub and cave can still be seen on the restricted hiking tour of Lower Vine Ranch. Scotty used the cave for refrigeration. Old-timers recall that after Scotty moved the tub outside, he could often be found sitting in a tub full of water in his long johns. Others remember that Scotty used it as his bed since he preferred the outdoors.

Scotty (left) enjoys a visit with an unidentified friend who is smoking a cigar while inside the central patio at the castle. The photograph was taken near the end of Scotty's life in 1953 by Tom G. Murray, who noted that "the two were watching the 'emo-grants' [tourists] as they visited the Castle."

Death Valley Scotty (right) sits across from one of his newspaper reporter friends, Bill Pique (left), as they engage in conversation in the great hall at the castle. An unidentified acquaintance looks on. The great hall, also known as the living room, was the most photographed room at the castle by visitors and invited guests alike.

BIBLIOGRAPHY

Buchel, Susan, and Robert Haile. *Scotty's Cook House Historic Structure Report.* Typed manuscript, Death Valley National Monument, July 1985.

Green, Linda Wedel. *Historic Furnishings Report Scotty's Castle: An Interior History of Death Valley Ranch.* Harpers Ferry: National Park Service, 1991.

Holland, F. Ross Jr. *Special Study Death Valley Scotty and Scotty's Castle.* Typed manuscript, Denver Service Center, Historic Preservation Team, National Park Service, United States Department of the Interior, Denver, CO, March 1973.

Johnston, Hank. *Death Valley Scotty "The Fastest Con in the West."* Corona del Mar: Trans-Anglo Books, 1974.

Lee, Bourke. *Death Valley Men.* New York: Macmillan Co., 1932.

Lingenfelter, Richard E. *Death Valley & The Amargosa.* Berkeley, CA: University of California Press, 1986.

National Park Service. *Cultural Landscape Inventory: Scotty's Castle.* Seattle, WA: National Park Service, 2005.

Palazzo, Robert P. *Darwin, California.* Lake Grove: Western Places, 1996.

———. *Death Valley.* Charleston, SC: Arcadia Publishing, 2008.

———. *Post Offices and Postmasters of Inyo County, California 1866–1966.* Fernley: Doug MacDonald, 2005.

Shally, Dorothy, and William Bolton. *Scotty's Castle.* Yosemite, CA: Flying Spur Press, 1973.

Visit us at
arcadiapublishing.com

•••